House Beautiful

Decorating with Fabric

Inspiring Sewing Projects for Every Room

The Editors of
House Beautiful Magazine

Gabi Tubbs

Text by Rhoda J. Murphy

With Photographs by Pia Tryde

Techniques and Projects Written
by Lucinda Ganderton

Illustrations by Alison Barratt

HEARST BOOKS

A Division of Sterling Publishing Co., Inc.

NEW YORK

Produced by Quadrille Publishing Limited, England.
Creative Director: Mary Evans
Editorial Director: Jane O'Shea
Art Director: Françoise Dietrich
Editors: Alexa Stace and Maggi McCormick
Design Coordinator: Sara Jane Glynn
Design Assistant: Nathalie Hennequin
Editorial Assistant: Katherine Seely
Production Manager: Candida Lane
Picture Researcher: Helen Fickling

Additional Text: Lucy Naylor

Library of Congress Cataloging-in-Publication Data
Available upon request.

10 9 8 7 6 5 4 3 2 1

First Paperback Edition 2003
Published by Hearst Books
A Division of Sterling Publishing Co., Inc.
387 Park Avenue South, New York, NY 10016

House Beautiful and Hearst Books are trademarks
owned by Hearst Magazines Property, Inc., in USA,
and Hearst Communications, Inc., in Canada.

www.housebeautiful.com

Distributed in Canada by Sterling Publishing
c/o Canadian Manda Group, One Atlantic Avenue, Suite 105
Toronto, Ontario, Canada M6K 3E7

Distributed in Australia by Capricorn Link (Australia) Pty. Ltd.
P.O. Box 704, Windsor, NSW 2756 Australia

Manufactured in China

ISBN 1-58816-297-4

contents

introduction

"There is no season such delight can bring

As summer, autumn, winter, and the spring."

So wrote Shakespeare contemporary William Basse. Many of us feel as Basse did,

that there is beauty to be found in every season. For others, it is the onset of a

particular season that makes their spirits rise—the joy of the first spring day, the

freedom of summer, a crisp day in autumn, or the sight of the world blanketed in

snow. Even if you live in an area where the seasonal changes are subtle, each time

of year has its own spirit.

Nothing evokes a particular mood more easily than fabrics. Think of putting on a

tweed blazer on the first chilly autumn day—suddenly you feel as if the season has

officially arrived. The same holds true for decorating. Certain fabrics and patterns

will conjure up a time of year. For instance, light floral cottons call to mind

spring, just as sumptuous velvets suggest winter cocooning. To simplify your

decorating, this book is organized by season. Each of the four chapters is full of

ways to bring the spirit of that particular time of year into your home. Every

chapter is interspersed with projects that have easy-to-follow instructions that will

help bring your rooms to life.

This book has two goals. The first is to help you find, in a sense, your decorating

personality—to help you identify the times of year that you love and to have your

home reflect those seasons. Secondly, it is to provide you with fabric tricks to make

you more comfortable—both physically and psychologically—in your home. For

example, on a hot summer day, it's a lot more appealing to stretch out on a sofa

covered in cotton pillows and slipcover than on wool upholstery. But most

important, the ideas in this book will help you to give your rooms personal style,

which in turn will be a true reflection of the family that lives there.

Knowing where to start when decorating or redecorating is always

a challenge, but the seasons offer strong precepts to organize

your decorating thoughts. Knowing your season can guide your

choices so that everything works in harmony. And by using fabrics,

you can impart a sense of season without a complete rehaul or

breaking the bank.

In spring, for example, we cannot wait to open doors and windows to let the light

and warmth come flooding in. This is when enthusiasm for decorating is in

plentiful supply. Carpets of spring flowers — bluebells, tulips, primroses — and trees

laden with blossoms all inspire a multitude of ideas. Fresh greens and radiant

pink ginghams are used with ticking stripes and floral prints.

Pink and yellow toiles de Jouy exist happily with checks.

In summer, decorating themes are unfussy. The feel is cool rather than cozy,

and your home should be clean and invigorating. Bring the outdoors into

your home with the colors of sea and sand, lush meadows, ripe juicy fruit and

bright splashy flowers. Allow the sun to find its way through white linen

blinds and billowing voile drapes.

In autumn, the countryside comes alive with purple hills, tawny trees and ripening

harvests in a splendid array of colors. Fabrics are reminiscent of scarlet leaves,

golden pumpkins, red berries and glowing heather and bracken. Soft traditional

tweeds and flannels jostle with bright tartans — fabrics that can be casual or

tailored. Think of them not confined solely to the country, but as equally

appealing in a city setting.

By the time we reach winter, when the weather is often cold and dreary, we want

energizing colors and touches of magic in the home to keep up our spirits. This is

the time for an abundance of opulent fabrics and rich color: decorate with velvets,

brocades and damasks; introduce exotic shades and fabrics inspired by the Far East,

like sheer muslins, silks and chiffons. For a more refined look, swathe furniture,

walls and windows in silvery grays and pearly whites.

This book is designed to rejuvenate and transform your home, as well as to inspire.

The designs have been carefully worked out, and are clearly illustrated with

straightforward instructions. And there are a few special designs for each season to

further encourage experimentation. Just as the seasons mirror nature's ever-

fascinating moods, decorating at its best reflects one's own changing taste.

spring
awakening

Who can resist the overwhelming sense of rebirth that arrives with spring? Not only does this season rouse the world of nature, it also sparks our desire to refresh, lighten and renew the rooms we live in. It is a time to edit down and simplify—there's a good reason why garage-sale season begins in April. But that air of rejuvenation goes well beyond the traditional spring cleaning. Now is the time to take down the heavy draperies and suspend a veil of delicate voile over the windows; to roll up the wool carpet; to throw open the windows and greet the outdoors.

natural inspiration

At the onset of spring, look no further than the garden

for design ideas. Each day brings new colors, patterns

and textures. All suggest decorating choices that can range

from such broad strokes as floor-sweeping toile window

panels to telling details, such as crisp table linens

easily sewn in an afternoon.

The photos on the following pages are packed with

suggestions for the season: paint your walls in atmospheric

pastels—pinks, lavenders, the palest blues, or a delicate

wash of green. Dress farmhouse chairs in bow-tied aprons;

adorn a plain-jane lamp with a gingham-covered shade.

And of course, fill your rooms with flowers—but resist the

impulse to overdo on floral fabrics. Remember, a bold flowery

print will have more impact when not

diluted by too many other florals.

Instead, complement it with solid colors,

awning stripes or engaging checks.

striking companions
to mix & match

Patterns and colors combine with seemingly reckless abandon in nature. The most appealing rooms also include a multitude of prints and hues. The secret lies in selecting one or two colors to dominate—then adding secondary colors for emphasis. Try pink and yellow, for example, with shots of purple for accent. You can always enlist the help of a color wheel—colors opposite each other are complementary. Or, look again to the outdoors—color combinations in nature will generally work indoors as well.

Pattern mixing is an inexact science. The typical designer "recipe" calls for a large-scale print, such as a floral chintz, as the primary pattern. Use it in a prominent place—covering a sofa, or for the draperies, then mix it with smaller prints. Plaids, checks, stripes, or a mini-toile can be layered with it, as long as each added print repeats at least two colors in the original pattern.

crisp & soft
textures for contrast

Just as juxtapositions of pattern and color bring a room to life, so do a variety of fabric textures. The most surprising combinations of textiles can bring out the best in each other when placed side by side. Delicate laces appear ethereal next to more earthbound cotton duck. Regal silks appear less lofty when teamed with unpretentious mattress ticking. Be sure to balance high-sheen fabrics that reflect light—such as polished chintzes and taffeta—with matte fabrics that absorb the light such as linens, cottons or wovens.

　　　Pick up samples (the larger the swatch the easier it will be to work with) of all the fabrics that catch your eye. Gather swatches together and mix and match. If they seem right together, chances are they will look so, too.

light affair

checks & toiles

in a garden room

STURDY TIES IN THE SAME BOLD LINEN CHECK AS

THE CUSHIONS ENSURE A NEAT LOOK ON A

VINTAGE CHAIR.

See pages 164–5 for gathered-corner cover.

It is hard to imagine a more perfect setting in which to enjoy a balmy spring morning than a garden room, bathed in natural light. If your home lacks such a space, change any sunny space into one—a screened or open porch, for example, or even the family room. In this spot, airiness and comfort reign. Unpretentious furniture is dressed in relaxed fabrics, and an antique sofa bed is piled with pillows, blatantly inviting idleness. The fabrics throughout the room are designed to evoke a spring garden party—fresh, pretty and engaging. Bold woven linen checks on an armchair call to mind picnic cloths; finely printed toiles recall the sweep of old-fashioned skirts brushing a lawn.

All clutter has been banished from walls and tabletops. Gardens are understated affairs in spring, and airy rooms should reflect that subtlety. Only a pair of wreaths break up the expanse of wall on one side, while a simple gilt mirror bounces light back into the room on the other wall. On the floor, pale, earthy tiles are ideal, in large part because of their practicality. But for those still-chilly mornings, a throw rug is a welcome addition.

right

SPRING COLORS COMBINE TO EVOKE THE SEASON.
HERE, PALE BLUE WALLS SET THE STAGE FOR GREEN
TOILE CURTAINS AND SWAGS TEAMED WITH PALE
YELLOWS AND ROSES ON AN ANTIQUE DAYBED.
**See pages 149 for unlined curtain, 146 for
soft roman shade, and 153 for swags.**

opposite

AN OLD BED SPEAKS OF COMFORT THANKS TO
PLENTY OF LOOSE PILLOWS DRESSED IN
LIGHTWEIGHT COTTON PRINTS.
**See pages 158–60 for pillows and 161–3
for bolsters.**

light & space
in sun-dappled rooms

This time of year light and airy spaciousness are prized. If your rooms lack such assets, you can create the illusion of them with a little decorating sleight of hand. Bare the windows so the sun can pour in or limit treatments to valances, loose swags or see-through sheer panels. Pare down the accessories and roll up the rugs—plain surfaces make spaces look bigger. Pack away the finery, take down the paintings and leave the walls bare. Maximize the light you do have with mirrors.

Above all, embrace simplicity. Blur the line between outdoors and inside spaces with garden pieces in wicker or wrought iron. And play up the rustic beauty of painted pieces with equally informal fabrics that don't detract from the furniture's country charm.

Play with patterns as well. Skilled decorators know well the power of pattern to make a room seem larger, smaller, sunnier or darker. To brighten a garden room, choose an abundance of delicate, small-scale designs rather than overpowering bold patterns. The smaller the pattern, the further away it seems to the eye, thereby visually increasing the sense of space in a room. Rely on solids for backdrops. Soft pastels or whites provide an unobtrusive backdrop for the lively informal fabrics of a garden room.

While perfectly matching rooms do lack life, a sense of unity should prevail. To achieve harmony, link details; for example, make a lampshade in the same fabric as a slipcovered chair, or repeat the floral print of the curtain in the ties on a cushion or pillow. A little discreet coordination goes a long way; too much is claustrophobic. The secret, not surprisingly, is balance.

THE FADED BLUE OF AN ANTIQUE PAINTED

BENCH IS ECHOED IN GLAZED WALLS AND A

TRADITIONAL SCANDINAVIAN BLUE-AND-CREAM-

CHECK CUSHION AND BOLSTER.

See pages 165 for fitted box cushion and

161–3 for bolsters.

A LOOSE FABRIC LAMPSHADE GIVES AN ORDINARY

LAMP DECORATIVE IMPACT.

See page 154 for lampshades.

An airy summer dress in smooth

Provençal cotton gives new life to a

plain wood chair.

See pages 168–9 for two-piece chair cover.

21

spring **awakening**

Quilted cotton place mats with

matching napkins are as practical as

they are attractive.

See page 185 for table linen.

A dining chair gets dressed in a

Sunday-best skirt and top sewn from

elegant chintz and taffeta.

See pages 168–9 for two-piece chair cover.

soft prints
for a garden setting

Dining al fresco is one of the joys of warm weather. Make a corner of the garden an outdoor "room" by carrying furniture outside for a special-occasion meal. Dress chairs for the day in ruffled skirts, and top the table with sprightly linens.

Afternoon tea, for example, becomes a grand event when served outdoors in a setting surrounded by flowers and greenery. The berry hues of jam and the soft hue of cream serve here as the inspiration for a scheme of lively floral prints, while the colors of cucumber sandwiches influenced the choice of thinly striped green and white taffeta for chairs. The chair coverings are deeply ruffled and tied with bows that bring to mind old-fashioned aprons.

By all means follow the colors of the flowers in your own garden, but add earthy shades and textures to balance the light hues. For added interest, vary the designs and fabrics of the chair covers.

A rough fabric such as a slubby linen makes a good rustic tablecloth, and plain cream-and-white china lets the fabric and centerpiece claim the attention. On a rainy day, bring it all indoors to create the atmosphere of a late spring garden. Or, if you are lucky enough to have a conservatory or garden room, recreate the setting in that space.

ON THE FIRST BALMY DAY OF SPRING, DINING TABLE (OR EVEN AN ORDINARY METAL FOLDING TABLE) AND CHAIRS ARE WHISKED OUTSIDE. THE TABLE WEARS A ROUGH LINEN TABLECLOTH WITH A SMALLER OVERCLOTH IN FLOWER-SPRIGGED COTTON, WITH QUILTED PLACE MATS TO MATCH. THE SKIRTED CHAIRS ARE SLIPCOVERED IN A COMBINATION OF CHINTZ AND TAFFETA.

See pages 184–5 for table linen.

A COMBINATION OF TIGHTLY RUCHED VALANCES AND UNLINED SWEDISH SHADES FILTER THE LIGHT IN THIS

SITTING ROOM. THE DUST RUFFLE ON THE IRON DAYBED IS ACTUALLY A SHORT CURTAIN WITH A GATHERED

HEADING ATTACHED TO THE BED FRAME.

See pages 145–6 for Swedish shade, 153 for ruffled valance and 151 for gathered heading.

For the picture bow see page 144.

sunny days

pastoral overtones
in a country sitting room

Printed with delicately rendered pastoral scenes, toile is perhaps the world's most romantic fabric pattern. It is also one of the most enduring: toile dates from the mid-17th-century. Traditionally executed in a single color on a cream background, the typical toile images of shepherds, 18th-century ladies, or animals seem quintessentially springlike. In this sitting room, a reproduction of an early toile pattern brings elegance to a pair of simple roll-up shades. Because privacy wasn't an important factor in this space, the shades were left unlined—their role is merely to lend softness and color to the long casement windows.

Although a room decorated entirely in toile has great appeal, one of the beauties of the fabric is its ability to add pattern to a room while still mixing easily with other toiles and prints. Toile and checks, in particular, are a classic combination. Here, tightly ruched valances in a taffeta check contrast with the filmy shades. Stripes, prints and more toile in the form of soft pillows and a deeply gathered bedskirt (gathers sewn with curtain header tape) bedeck the antique iron daybed. The rich melange of patterns works because it echoes the petal pink of the walls and buttercup yellow shades. A bare floor keeps the multitude of colors and patterns from overwhelming the room.

PILLOWS ARE AN EASY WAY TO ADD OR SUBDUE PATTERN. A MIX OF PILLOWS GIVES THIS DAYBED ITS STYLE.

See pages 155–63 for pillows, cushions, and bolsters.

THIS LAMP ACHIEVES GLAMOUR WITH A SILKY TAFFETA "OVERSKIRT" THAT TOPS A MATCHING SHADE BENEATH.

See page 154 for gathered lampshade.

made to measure **a cover for a storage unit**

Extra closet space has never had more flair than does this tented wardrobe or shelf unit. For the "dress" we used an architectural toile named Les Vues de Paris, while for the top and shelves, we opted for a less defined complementary toile. The scalloped shelf lining is fixed to the wooden shelves with Velcro®. The whole tent slips easily over the unit and can be removed for drycleaning or careful washing. A matching cord is threaded through a buttonhole in the side seams and ties back the front curtains on either side. The wired topknot adds a quirky touch. The height of the roof can be altered to fit the proportions of your room by changing the length of the wooden struts.

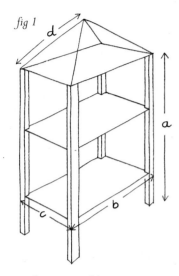

fig 1

materials

Main fabric (x = 60″ wide), contrast fabric, lining fabric, wooden shelf unit (approx 72″ high, 45″ wide, 20″ deep), 4 lengths of ¼″ x ¾″ wooden strips (28″ long) for struts, masking tape, drill, strong twine, 4 screws, 6″ x 16½″ fusible bonding web, 1yd. millinery wire, 6yd. thick cord for tiebacks, thumbtacks, craft knife, Velcro (18″ per shelf), craft glue

measuring & cutting out *(figs 1 & 2)*

Allow extra fabric to match repeats (see p.148). Add ¾″ all around each piece. NB: z equals 2″.

from main fabric

Side curtain: cut two, width = x (60″), length = a + 5z (10″)

Back curtain: cut one, width = y (45″), length = a + 5z (10″)

Facings: cut two, width = 8″, length = a + 10″

from contrast fabric

Main roof: cut two, sides of triangle = d, width = b, border height = 4z (8″)

Side roof: cut two, sides of triangle = d, width = c, border height = 4z (8″). Notch the sides of each roof piece, 2″ below the point

Shelf cover: cut one for each shelf, width = b, depth = c + 2z (4″)

Shelf facings: cut one for each shelf, width = b, depth = 2z (4″)

Top knot: cut one, 11″ x 33″

from lining fabric

Roof facings: cut two, width = 4z (8″), length = b

Side roof facings: cut two, width = (8″), length = c

making the roof framework

1 Assemble the unit as instructed. Drill a ¼″ hole ⅜″ from one end of each wooden strip. Drill a ⅛″ hole 1″ in from the other end. Thread string through the large holes. Knot securely, but loosely enough for the struts to move freely. Tape the frame in position on the top of the unit and mark the points where the struts meet uprights. Drill into the uprights at the correct angle, then screw the frame in place *(fig 3)*.

making the curtain

2 Zigzag one long edge of each facing. With right sides together, pin and stitch the unstitched edges to the outside edges of the side curtains. Press the seam toward the facing. Turn facing to the wrong side of curtain. If you are using a nonreversible fabric, put the curtain together so that the right side of the back piece faces forward. Pin and stitch the right side of each side piece to the wrong side of the back, matching the raw edges. Turn up a 4″ hem (equal loops) along the lower edge.

3 With a thumbtack, secure the center back of the curtain to the center back of the top shelf and the top corners to the center front. Make three small pleats on each side of the opening and attach to the shelf with tacks. Fold and pin a 6″ inverted

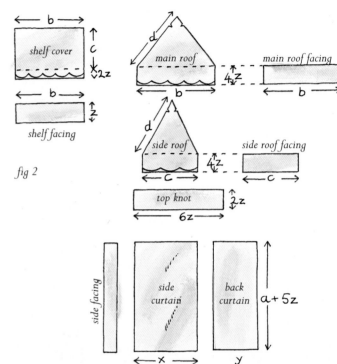

fig 2

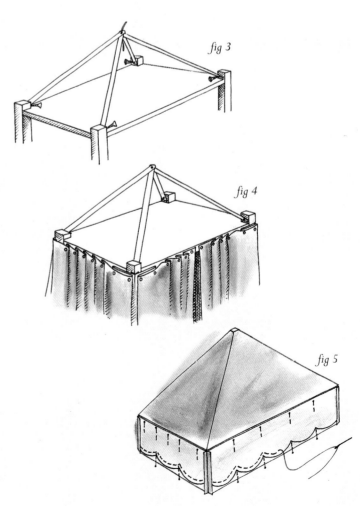

fig 3

fig 4

fig 5

box pleat at each front corner. Pin the side seams to the back corners and then fold and pin the remaining loose fabric in small pleats *(fig 4)*.

making the roof

4 With right sides together, pin one side roof to each side of one main roof piece along short and diagonal edges. Stitch from notch to ¾" from lower edge, making a ¾" seam. Join second main roof piece to the two free sides. Press seams.

5 Pin one side roof facing to each end of one main roof facing, then pin the remaining main piece to the loose ends. Stitch ¾" from the edges, and press the seams flat. Finish one edge. Mark three shallow scallops along the other edge of the side facings and five along the roof facings, following the method on page 156.

6 Pin the facing to the bottom edge of the roof with right sides together, matching the corners. Baste together close to the scallops *(fig 5)* and stitch along the line. Trim and clip the curves and points (see p.139). Turn right side out and press. Pin the free edge of the facing to the roof fabric.

making the top knot

7 Join the short ends with right sides together and press the seam open. Fold in half lengthwise with wrong sides together. Press and open out again. Lay the bonding web on the wrong side of one half of the loop and press *(fig 6)*. Peel off the backing paper and fold again along the crease. Twist the ends of the millinery wire together to form a ring the same size as the fabric loop. Place the wire inside the fold and pin it in place. Press the fabric to bond the two sides together. Using a zipper foot, stitch along the fold, close to the wire.

8 Carefully bend the loop into a series of pleats, and pin them together at the lower edge *(fig 7)*. Slip pinned edge of the topknot into the hole at the top of the roof and adjust the pleats so that it fits tightly. Remove and slipstitch each pleat in place 1¼" from the lower edge. Pin back onto the roof and stitch firmly in place.

9 Drop the roof over its frame so that the scallops hang over the top edge of the curtain. Match the corners, then pin the roof to the curtain through the facing, adjusting pleats to fit. With the curtain pleats pinned to the roof, carefully remove unit. Topstitch all around twice. Return tent to shelf.

10 Hang a tieback cord around the front upright next to the center shelf. Mark the point where it will come through on the inside of the box pleat and remove the tent. Cut a 2½" square of fabric and press under ¼" along each edge. Draw a long oval on the wrong side, large enough for the cord to pass through easily. Pin the patch to the mark with right sides together and stitch around the mark. Clip into the opening *(fig 8)* and turn the patch to the wrong side. Press, pin in place, and topstitch the edges to secure. Repeat at the other front upright.

making the shelf covers

11 Face and make five scallops at one b edge as for roof. Hem the remaining sides. Cut short strips of Velcro and separate. Sew four pieces to the wrong side of each back edge at intervals. Stick the other pieces to the shelves to correspond.

12 Position all covers, then put the tent back on the frame. Loop the tiebacks around the uprights, thread through the openings, and knot the ends loosely.

fig 6

fig 7

fig 8

creating a sanctuary

details transform
a simple bedroom

A FABRIC SCREEN OFFERS FLEXIBLE PRIVACY AND DOUBLES AS ART. TO MAKE IT, GATHER A FABRIC PANEL TO THE TOP AND BOTTOM WITH CURTAIN-HEADER TAPE, THEN ATTACH TO A WOODEN FRAME SCREEN WITH MATCHING TIES.

See pages 151 for gathered heading and 144 for ties.

Decorating inspiration can come from many sources—usually it flows from a particular fabric, a rug or piece of furniture. But occasionally, one tiny feature in a room can serve as the decorative jumping-off point. Such was the case in this small bedroom. Here, an old gilded tieback was the starting point for a decorating scheme that calls to mind the faded charm of an old French manor house, where hints of bygone opulence mingle with homespun fabrics and objects. One plus of such a technique: it helps give a space true personal style.

While you may use a detail to set the theme in a bedroom, keep comfort foremost in your mind. Once you've decided on a decorating approach, dress the bed first and plan the rest of the room around it. In a small space, echo the bed's patterns and colors throughout the room, to avoid strong contrasts that would make the bed become too dominant a feature. That does not mean you must limit yourself to only one pattern. As long as you link your prints through their colors, several designs can work harmoniously without making the room appear too busy. Here, the green of a nostalgic toile is picked up by a contemporary gingham. And the deep red edges of the petals in a floral cotton match a pink-and-cream glazed cotton check. Fabrics of different textures are mixed as well to add interest and a sense of layering to the space.

THE WORN FINISH OF AN ANTIQUE GILDED TIE-BACK COMPLEMENTS OLD-FASHIONED TOILE CURTAINS.

A BED MAKES A STRONG STATEMENT WHEN COVERED WITH GRAY TOILE AND GREEN GINGHAM.
See page 182 for tie-on duvet cover.

Restful grays and greens create an air of repose in this guest bedroom. Though the prints differ, they complement each other. The gingham trim of the duvet matches the scalloped cushion as well as the dust ruffle. Gingham bows dress the footstool cover, made from a square of fabric, slightly gathered at the corners.

See pages 156 for scalloped-edge cover, 183 for gathered dust ruffle and 181 for footstool cover with bows.

WHEN SPRING BREEZES BLOW, THESE TRANSLUCENT TOILE PANELS BILLOW. THE LIGHTWEIGHT COTTON SHADES ADD ANOTHER DELICATE ELEMENT TO THE WINDOWS.

See pages 146 for soft roman shade and 149 for unlined curtains.

SPRINGTIME MEANS BABIES! THIS LAYETTE BASKET IS LINED SIMILARLY TO THE MOSES BASKET **(on pages 134–7)** BUT HAS AN EXTRA TOUCH—PLENTY OF POCKETS TO HOLD BABY TOILETRIES.

spring greens & blossom pinks
for finishing touches

Generous amounts of fabric lend a sense of comfort to a bedroom. Inexpensive fabrics can have as great an impact as costly ones. Here's a trick: use inexpensive cotton checks and stripes for the large pieces—the dust ruffle, duvet cover and slipcovers—then splurge on more elegant fabrics for the small touches. The combination of the simple with the splendid will bring out the best in each.

  Although a workaday ticking fabric covers this chair, the details are all glamour. Both the frilled piping and bows are sewn from pricey silk taffeta—left over from a pair of curtains. The footstool's generous bows are also made from the same fabric. Pillows are yet another way to mix the mundane with the luxurious. Stitch up pillows in silk or taffeta remnants and trim them with cottons—or try the reverse.

PINK TAFFETA BOWS EMBELLISH A LOOSE-FITTING

SLIPCOVER SEWN FROM COTTON TICKING.

passion for red

bold sophistication
in a master bedroom

Red is one of nature's most glorious colors. If you love wearing red, then indulge that passion for red in rooms. Although red interiors are usually associated with the winter holidays, there's no reason why red can't evoke spring. Think of a late spring garden, full of poppies and peonies, rhododendrons and camelias. Carry those deep pinks and reds in your head to choose fabrics that will recreate that freshness.

If solid red walls seem like too much for you, choose patterns that are offset by an abundance of creamy tones. Red and ivory toile, for example, lets you indulge a passion for red without making your bedroom impossible to sleep in. Toile works best, however, if used as the dominant pattern in a master bedroom. Mix contemporary interpretations with reproductions of original designs, using varying shades of reds and pinks as long as all have the same background color. For visual interest opt for varying weights and textures.

Lavish toiles on the bed, sofas, chairs, curtains, cushions, wall hangings and dressing-table—anything that can be draped. For the most sumptuous-looking room, follow the philosophy of "the more the merrier." Do, however, keep your primary surfaces—ceiling and floor—in neutral colors to offset the richness of the red and the drama of the toiles.

opposite

TO BRING UNITY TO THIS MASTER SUITE, THE
RED TOILE EXTENDS INTO THE BATHROOM.
A CIRCULAR TABLE IS COVERED WITH A
TRIMMED ROUND CLOTH TOPPED BY A
SQUARE OVER-CLOTH.

See page 184 for tablecloths.

right

QUILTING EMPHASIZES THE PLAYFUL SCENES ON
THE TOILE THAT MAKE UP THE BEDSPREAD FOR
THIS MASTER BEDROOM. THE PILLOWCASES AND
LINED BED CURTAINS ARE IN THE SAME RED HUES
BUT WITH DIFFERENT PICTORIALS. THE BEDSIDE
TABLECLOTH IS SEWN LIKE A CIRCULAR PLACE MAT
AND TRIMMED WITH CORD PIPING AND A
RUFFLED EDGE.

**See pages 38–9 for outline-quilted
bedspread and drapes, 155–7 for
pillowcases.**

coronet **for a luxurious bedroom**

What could be more elegant than a bed topped with a canopy and coronet? Rich folds of fabric that extend to the ceiling make the canopy a private room within a room. Here, antique French brass bows and swags decorate the velvet-covered coronet.

The double-sided quilt has a delicate toile design on the underside that creates a contrast with the busier outside toile.

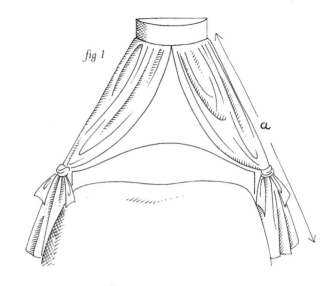

fig 1

materials

for the curtains & tiebacks

Main fabric (60″ wide), contrasting fabric, fringed braid (length = 60″, + 2a + 6 fabric widths), chalk pencil or fading pen, 50 curtain hooks, 6yd. covered narrow piping cord, 2 small brass rings, 2 cup hooks

for the coronet

Semicircle of 1″ blockboard (19″ in diameter), contrasting fabric, white glue, awl, 50 eye screws, 2 angle brackets with screws, 60″ x 4″ mounting board, 26″ x 60″ velvet, 1¾yd x ⅜″-wide velvet-covered piping cord, upholstery tacks, additional trim as desired

measuring & cutting out *(figs 1 & 2)*

The coronet is mounted on the wall above the center of the bed; the height will depend on the proportions of your room. Decide where it should go before calculating fabric amounts. Allow extra fabric to match repeats (see p.148). NB: z equals width of fabric: this can vary between 48″ and 60″.

Back curtain: cut one from main and one from contrasting fabric width = 3 widths of fabric, length = a + 1½″
Side curtains: cut two from main and two from contrasting fabric width = 1.5 widths of fabric, length = a + 1½″
Tiebacks: cut two from main and contrasting fabric width = (x) = 6″, length = 60″

Coronet lining: cut a 24″ semicircle from contrasting fabric
Valance cover: cut from velvet, width (x) = 6″, length (y)= 60″

making the coronet

1   Cover the underside the blockboard with contrasting fabric, pull it tightly over the edges and glue. Make a row of small holes, 1½″ apart, ½″ in from the entire outside edge with an awl, leaving a 4″ gap at the center front. Screw an eye into each hole, twisting it until secure, so that the eye lies parallel to the edge. Mount the two angle brackets to the top of the board, each 5″ in from the edge.
2   Cover the mounting board with velvet, and hand stitch or glue the covered piping along the long top edge, finishing the ends. Bend the lower edge gently around the curved edge of the board and anchor with tacks *(fig 3)*. Glue on the fringed braid to cover the tacks. Add any further decoration at this stage, then screw the board in place on the wall.

making the curtains

1   Cut the selvages from the main curtain fabric. Join widths together as on p.143, then join back and side curtains, repeat with the contrasting fabric and make one large curtain by the bagging method (see p.143). Stitch the fringed braid to the right side along the seamed edges. Press under ¾″ along both sides of the top edge and topstitch together.
2   Hand-stitch pencil pleats along the top of the curtain, to draw width up to

fig 2

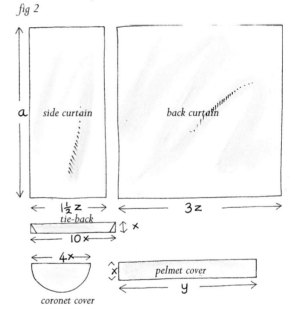

fig 3

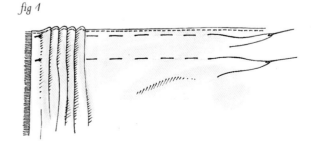

fig 4

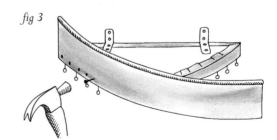

2¼ yards in the following manner. Mark two lines, ½″ and 2″ from top on wrong side. Thread two strong needles with double lengths of buttonhole thread and secure one at the beginning of each line, 1½″ in from edge. Sew ¾″ running stitches along both lines, drawing up fabric at intervals and fastening off tightly before starting a new length *(fig 4)*. Continue to within 1½″ of the end. Sew curtain hooks concealed inside folds with just tips showing, at 1½″ intervals.

3 Pin the two pieces of each tieback together at the ends, then cut corners at an angle. Pin and stitch a round of piping to right side of each contrasting fabric piece, then with right sides together, pin each main fabric piece in place. Sew each tieback together, just inside previous stitch line, leaving a 2″ opening in the center of one long edge. Clip corners and turn right side out. Press and slipstitch opening closed. Sew a brass ring to center of each tie on main fabric side.

4 Hang up the curtain, starting at the center front and slotting one hook through each screw eye. Mount a cup hook on each side of the bed at the height where the tiebacks will hang. Mark the seams between the back and side curtains at this height. Take down the curtains and undo the seam on both sides of the curtain for 3″ on each side of the mark. Slipstitch the front to the back along the previous stitch line to form a slot. Hang the tiebacks on the wall and re-hang the curtains. Pass one end of each tieback through the slots and tie loosely.

outline quilted bedspread

materials & equipment

Main fabric, contrasting fabric, solid fabric, batting, walking foot for sewing machine, quilter's safety pins, quilter's clips

measuring and cutting out (fig 1)

Front: cut one from main fabric, width = a, length = 2b, + 1¼″ all around
Backing: cut one from contrasting fabric, as front
Batting: cut one, as front, joining widths with a loose herringbone stitch
Binding: cut a 3¼″ strip from solid fabric, length = 2a + 2b + 16″.

making

1 Lay the batting flat over muslin and place the front piece on top, right side up. Join layers together with basting or quilter's safety pins. Take time to do this, smoothing the fabric as you go. Work from the center out to the four corners, then to the middle of each side. Continue making parallel lines 10″ apart, to cover the whole surface *(fig 2)*. When finished, roll up the sides and hold in place with quilter's clips, leaving a 16″ area on which to work *(fig 3)*.

2 Decide in advance which areas to quilt. Using a medium straight stitch, sew slowly and steadily along the fabric design outlines. When complete, re-roll the sides to expose the next section. Work from the center out to each side in turn.

3 Tie off the loose threads on the wrong side. Trim and square up the edges. Pin the backing, right side out, to the front. Stitch together, ⅜″ from the edge, then bind (see p.140).

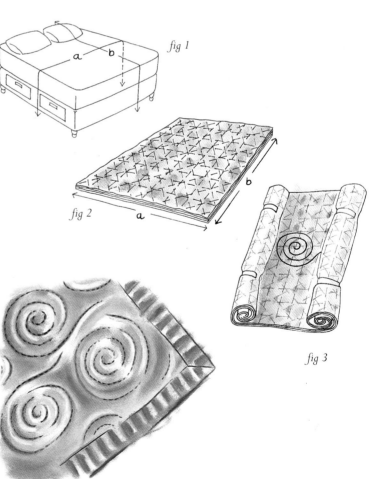

fig 1

fig 2

fig 3

spring **awakening**

right

FRENCH PAINTED FURNITURE, DECORATIVE
ACCESSORIES AND DELICATE CHINA—ALL FROM
THE 17ᵀᴴ AND 18ᵀᴴ-CENTURIES—ENHANCE FABRIC
DESIGNS FROM THE SAME PERIOD. A GLORIOUS
COTTON PRINT CURTAIN SETS THE ELEGANT SCENE.

See page 149 for loose-lined curtains.

SCATTER CUSHIONS IN TOILES AND CHECKS,
TRIMMED GENEROUSLY WITH FRINGING, BOBBLES,
TIES AND ROPE, LOOK ALMOST SCULPTURAL WHEN
PILED HIGH ON A PAINTED STOOL.

See pages 158–60 for pillows and 166 for

footstool cushion.

opulent fabrics
make a boudoir

Nothing adds elegance to a room quite like windows cloaked in floor-sweeping cascades of fabric. In general, the longer the drapery and the greater the puddle of fabric, the more formal the look. To create a generous puddle, add an extra six inches to the finished length of your draperies. If practical considerations—children or pets—prohibit very long window treatments, add only an extra inch or two. To get the look of lavish window treatments without splurging on yards of fabric, make the curtain panels stationary and suspend them on a rod on either side of the window. Add a shade or blinds for light control and privacy. In order to maximize the amount of light your room receives, hang your window treatments outside the confines of the window, so that when draperies are opened the flow of light is maximized.

But by no means should you confine a love of fabrics to curtains. There are limitless possibilities for fabric. For instance, you can use fabric to turn a humdrum bookshelf into an eye-catching piece. Simply line the shelves with upholstery fabric (or wallpaper) adding three or four inches of overhang. Add an interesting touch by snipping the overhang into scallops or points.

AN ORDINARY CUPBOARD BECOMES AN OBJECT OF BEAUTY WHEN THE SHELVES ARE LINED WITH TOILE. THE SCALLOPED EDGE MAKES A LIVELY AND APPEALING ACCENT.

summer
lightness

It's summertime and the decorating is easy. Now life is simpler;

schedules and shoes go bye the bye. Put your home in a summer state

of mind by making it reflect that ease. Replace your rugs with beach-

evoking sisal. Pack away formality—the good china, the silver, the

delicate accessories—and put out rustic baskets or terra-cotta

planters filled with flowers. Bring the outdoors in and vice versa, and turn any outside

space—the garden, the terrace, or even a balcony—into an extension of your home.

natural inspiration

With nature at its most verdant, design

inspiration lies at almost every turn.

Think of your favorite summer

sanctuary—the beach, the woods, or

even your own garden—and evoke it

with colors, fabrics and objects.

Paint your walls the rich green of summer leaves,

then dress your sofa and chairs in airy white slipcovers.

Bring wicker furniture indoors and spruce it up with

cushions and pillows covered in flowery cottons. Little

touches can also make a statement—even something as

simple as decorating a cocktail table with a bowl full of

shells will remind you of the sea.

brilliant hues
for summer effects

The summer season abounds with strong color—the brilliant hues of late season flowers; the blues and grays of the seaside; the deep greens of forests; the pure white of high summer clouds. Bid adieu to the pastels of spring; warm weather hues are vivid. Stronger sunlight enables you to use bold hues that would overpower in the faint light of winter. The brilliant citrus colors of the Caribbean look especially appealing on a hot day. Indulge a love of gutsy yellows, limes and orange—just make sure that all have the same intensity so they don't clash. Temper them and other brilliant colors with an abundance of white and natural shades. Bold solids, crisp stripes or large checks all reflect summer, as do overscaled flower prints. Alternatively, turn to white. No color can match white's ability to open up spaces and highlight a room's character. And nothing else feels quite so cool on a steamy day as an all-white room. White needn't be impractical. Opt for washable whites, such as polyester voile curtains, cotton duck slipcovers, and even white cotton sheets. When choosing whites, heed the advice of New York designer Robert K. Lewis. As he once told *House Beautiful*, "Several whites are always more interesting than one. But beware of the white that turns bluish. It can have a cold look."

airy & crisp
textures for contrast

Put away or cover up the velvets and wools; summer's textures are airy and light. Especially if you are decorating your rooms in neutral colors or are creating an all-white scheme, look to texture to create interest and style. Light-as-air cottons are a given, making sheets an ideal choice for decorating projects. Crisp *broderie anglaise* also projects coolness. Mix your cottons with a combination of linens—slubby natural and fine smooth linen—for pillows, slipcovers and table skirts. Hang translucent sheers—voiles or batistes—at the window. Loosely wrap them around a wooden or iron rod as an informal window scarf, or drape them over a table as a see-through skirt.

Grasses add another element—put woven wood blinds at the windows, inexpensive reed mats on the floor. The best aspect of all these summer textures is their practicality. The fabrics are easily washable, the blinds inexpensive, and the mats can be picked up and shaken out.

FABRIC COVERS BRING SUMMER BEAUTY TO OUTDOOR FURNISHINGS. AN ANTIQUE COTTON CURTAIN

ENVELOPS A SIMPLE ROUND TABLE, WHILE OTHER COTTON PRINTS UNIFY A COLLECTION OF GARDEN CHAIRS.

See pages 158–60 for pillows, 166 for frilled cushion for basket chair, and 167

for tie-on cushion.

under a greenwood tree

abundant flowers
for a lazy afternoon

The flowers of summer tend to be big and showy—think of overblown roses, voluptuous peonies, stately lilies. The grand floral displays of the season offer as good a reason as any for setting up camp in the garden. But you could recreate that freshness of color indoors as well. Try a sky blue for the walls or for an old piece of furniture and bring it to life with colorful stencils. Alternatively, clad your walls in pale washed hues and put up decorative shelves to house pots of geraniums or marigolds. To decorate a porch or sun-room, use the hues of your garden for inspiration. The room will become a lovely transitional space between outside and in. Or, imagine your dream garden and choose the colors and textures that best reflect its characteristics. You will then have the perfect setting for idyllic summer lounging. And when the blooms in the garden have long since faded, the flower-scattered fabrics will be a delightful reminder of sunny days and balmy nights.

ROSES ON DUSKY PINK AND WHITE COTTON REQUIRE THE UNASHAMEDLY

FEMININE FINISH OF GATHERED EDGES AND BOWS.

scattered posies
for a garden room

Summerizing a room is easy with plenty of room-cheering fabrics. Soft faded cottons, sheer voiles or crisp white lawn are instant sunshine. Make chair covers from delicate floral prints to slip over heavy, wintry upholstery. Drape dark wood tables with cotton and linen prints and cover a lamp with a matching or complementary fabric. The beauty of this type of decorating is that nothing need fit exactly. Looseness implies comfort.

Don't be restrained in your choice of florals—the more lush the better. Big blooms are part of the glory of summer. Mix dainty florals with bolder ones—just as long as the colors are the same. The fruits of summer provide yet another theme—cherries, apples, and grapes. Give your creations a finished look with piping, ribbons, or scalloped edges

Cushions and pillows are an inexpensive way to change the mood of a room. Pile them high on a sofa, a wooden bench, or rattan chair. Or soften the appearance of metal or wooden folding chairs with tie-on seats or backs. Use remnants to make simple drawstring bags or line baskets to hold sewing necessities. Extra fabric pieces can also be used to mat inexpensive prints—just glue the fabric onto stiff cardboard, then surround it with an inexpensive frame.

For a dining room, bring out the colors in your china by choosing linens that echo its pattern, or pick up one or two colors, and sew a set of napkins and place mats from them. And don't fold them away into drawers when not in use: pile them on a sideboard as an accent.

right & opposite

A FRILLY LAMPSHADE AND A MATCHING DRAWSTRING BAG ECHO THE PINK HUES IN AN ARMCHAIR'S LOOSE SLIPCOVER. THE COVER IS SECURED AT THE BACK OF THE CHAIR WITH APPEALING FABRIC BOWS.

See pages 178–80 for tie-backed chair cover and 154 for ruffled lampshade.

left

A BASKET OF CHERRIES SERVED AS THE

INSPIRATION FOR THE FABRIC USED HERE IN LUSH

SUMMER PILLOWS, CUSHIONS, AND SOFT QUILTS.

See pages 158–160 for pillows.

below

YELLOW GINGHAM TRIM ACCENTS A BLUE-AND-

PINK DRAWSTRING BAG AND A MOSES BASKET.

fabric folly for a summer canopy & stools

A summer house to sit and dream in is a luxury out of reach for most people. Here's a way that you can have that fantasy. Next time you are planning your ideal garden, complete with gazebo, consider constructing a canopy instead. It's equally blissful, but much easier to realize. All you need is a fabric roof—scalloped in the style of a medieval tent—with sides that can be rolled or hitched up to let in light and air. Choose a cotton that repeats the colors of a nearby border or hedge. Cover garden stools for the interior in a complementary fabric.

Putting the framework of the canopy together is a family effort, as three people are needed to assemble the parts. Do this before sewing the cover, so that you can check for a perfect fit.

materials & equipment
for the frame

2 x 1¼″ poles (12″ long) for the vertical roof struts, 3 x 1¼″ poles (8′ long) for the long horizontal roof struts, 2 x 1¼″ poles (5′ long) for the short horizontal roof struts, 4 x 1¼″-diameter poles (6½′ long) for the uprights, roll of heavy-duty adhesive tape, 4 x 3-way corner connectors, 2 x T-connectors, 2 x right-angle connectors, Allen wrench, 4 long nails, 4 x 8′ long lengths of strong string, 4 tent stakes, chisel, drill

for the canopy

Main fabric, contrasting fabric, thin cardboard, chalk pencil or fading pen

for the stools

Small folding stool, main fabric, ¾″ upholstery tacks and hammer

making the frame

1 Chisel down one end of each upright to make it fit into the 3-way corner connector. Drill a hole in the other end and hammer in a nail to make a spike.

2 Wrap two layers of tape around both ends of each roof pole. Thread the T-connectors onto the short horizontal struts. Position them centrally, with the empty connection facing up, and tighten the nuts with the Allen wrench. Push the taped ends of the short and two of the long horizontal struts into the 3-way connectors to make a rectangular frame and tighten.

3 Push one end of each vertical strut into an empty T-connector. Put a right-angle connector on each end of the remaining long roof pole and tighten. Push the free ends of the right-angle connectors onto the vertical struts and tighten.

4 Lay the roof frame out on the ground where the canopy will stand. Mark each corner with a stake and use these as a guide to plant the uprights firmly in the lawn. Tie a loop in both ends of each piece of string to make guy lines. Loop one over the top of each upright so that the loop rests on the flange. Lift the roof and place the empty sockets of the 3-way corner connectors over the top of the uprights and tighten *(fig 1)*. Stretch out the strings and stake down.

making the canopy

measuring & cutting out *(figs 1 & 2)*

Add ¾″ all around each piece except the ties. The shaded areas represent fabric that will be cut away. NB: z equals 8″ in the cutting instructions below.

from main fabric

Main roof: cut two, width = b, depth = a + z (8″)
Side roof: cut two, width = d, depth = c + z (8″)
Side panels: cut two, width = d, length = e + z (8″)

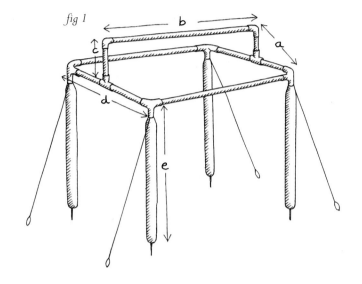

fig 1

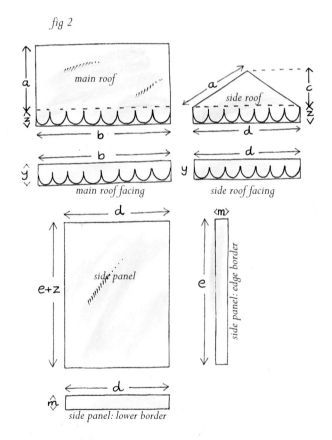

fig 2

main roof

side roof

main roof facing

side roof facing

side panel

side panel: edge border

side panel: lower border

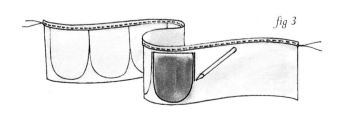

fig 3

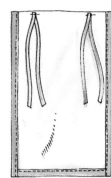

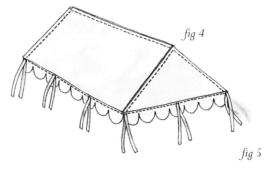

fig 4

from contrast fabric

Main roof facing: cut two, width = y (8¾"), length = b

Side roof facing: cut two, width = y (8¾"), length = d

Side panel edge border: cut four, width = m (5½"), length = e

Side panel lower border: cut two, width = m (5½"), length = d

Ties: cut ten strips, 6 x 12"; Panel ties: cut 4 strips, 14 x 2 yd

fig 5

finishing

1 Make a template for the scallops by subtracting 1½" from length d and dividing by seven. Cut a piece of cardboard this width by 7". Draw a deep scallop shape and cut out. Make a ⅜" double hem along the top edge of one side roof facing. Starting ¾" in from the side and matching the top to the hem fold, draw around the template seven times or to make the desired number of scallops *(fig 3)*.

2 With right sides together, pin the facing strip to the lower edge of the side roof. Baste close to scallop line, then stitch. Trim and clip the curves and points (see p.139). Turn right side out and press. Stitch the hemmed edge of the facing to the main fabric. Do the same with the other side roof, and make an edging of eight scallops along the lower edge of the main roof pieces in the same way.

3 With right sides together, pin and stitch the two main roof pieces together along the top edge, making a ¾" seam. Pin and stitch the side roof pieces to each end. Make the ties as on p.144. Fold them in half and sew one securely to each corner, one to the center lower edge of each side roof, and two, evenly spaced, to the lower edge of each main roof piece *(fig 4)*.

4 Press under ⅜" along long edges of each panel border, and, wrong sides together, press each border in half lengthwise. Pin and stitch one short strip over lower edge of each side panel like a binding. Press under ⅜" at lower end of each long border. Pin and stitch down the sides, so folded end lies along hem line.

5 Make the panel ties as on p.144. Fold in half and pin to the top of the side panels, 15" in from each edge. Pin the upper edge of each panel in position against the hemmed scalloped roof edge, with the right side facing out. and stitch in place, catching in the panel ties *(fig 5)*. Tie the canopy onto the frame.

making the stools

measuring & cutting out

Seat: remove the existing cover. Use it as a guide to cut a rectangle the same length by twice the width, plus 1¼".

Ruffle: cut two 4" strips, length = twice the width of the seat

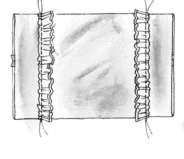

fig 6

finishing

1 Fold seat piece in half crosswise, right sides together. Pin, stitch ⅝" from edge opposite fold. Press seam flat, turn right side out. Press seam along center back.

2 Make a narrow double hem along sides and one long edge of each ruffle piece. Gather raw edge to fit width of seat (see p.142). Mark where seat folds over frame. With right sides facing, pin and stitch ruffles along these lines, with finished edges facing center *(fig 6)*. Tack cover to underside of wooden frame.

An inexpensive metal or wood folding table

becomes a setting worthy of a wedding,

thanks to a flowing floral table skirt

trimmed on the corners with puffy bows.

See pages 184–5 for fitted buffet

tablecloth and 144 for bows.

table manners
frocks for furniture

The Victorian obsession that saw chairs and tables covered with floor-gracing fabric stemmed from a general feeling in polite society that the sight of chair and table legs was unseemly. Just as arms and legs were swathed in long skirts, so furniture was kept under wraps. The result of this over-attention to morals was imaginative fabric creations for chairs, trestle tables, dressing tables and side tables.

Revive these niceties for either indoors or out. For a gracious garden party, drape a folding table in a light fabric in colors that call to mind strawberries and cream, Victoria plums and ripe cherries. Choose smooth cotton or shiny chintz that is heavy enough to fold elegantly where it hits the floor. Lift the tablecloth a few inches at each corner to reveal a daring, snowy white "petticoat" undercloth sewn from either linen, *broderie anglaise*, or a white cotton sheet. Emphasize the corners by pinning or sewing on four generous bows. Just be sure that the fabric is stiff enough that the bows will not droop.

DAINTY PINK-AND-WHITE CHECKS COMPLEMENT A ROSY FLORAL FOR A DRESSING TABLE AND MATCHING STOOL. PIPING DEFINES THE CURVES OF THE DRESSING TABLE. TO STITCH THESE TWO PROJECTS, FOLLOW THE INSTRUCTIONS GIVEN FOR THE WOOL PLAID VERSION OF THIS PROJECT.
(see pages 184–5).

subtle charm
garden dressings

In warm weather, garden furniture deserves the same care and attention we usually devote to a living room. Make your time outside as enjoyable as possible by turning a corner of the yard into an inviting spot for leisure. Let your particular style of outdoor furniture guide you when selecting fabrics. Wide-armed rattan or wicker pieces gain added appeal from strong awning stripes or wide checks. Natural or painted wooden benches and tables can be teamed with plain linens, either in bright or neutral colors or sharp geometric patterns. You can even do a decorating makeover on inexpensive plastic furniture with cushions and pillows in eye-catching fabrics. The most romantic of all garden furniture—old wrought-iron—looks irresistible when partnered with faded flowery chintzes.

There's a natural appeal to faded fabrics. To find them, scour flea markets, estate sales or even garage sales for old draperies, tablecloths or even vintage dresses to sew into covers, chair seats, pillows or just for decorative bows. One caveat: be sure to launder your finds before making them up into new furnishings. Where changes in color occur, usually in seam allowances or hems, either cut around them, or make the discolorations look deliberate—as part of the charm.

opposite

OLD-FASHIONED VICTORIAN WROUGHT IRON GAINS EXTRA GLAMOUR FROM OLD CHINTZES AND A VASE OF ENGLISH ROSES.

right

MAKE THE MOST OF LEFTOVER FABRIC OR A SMALL PIECE OF A VINTAGE TEXTILE, TO SEW A LINING FOR A SMALL BASKET.

far right

SEAT CUSHIONS TIE ONTO CHAIRS FOR QUICK REMOVAL SHOULD A SUNNY DAY TURN STORMY.

See page 167 for tie-on cushion.

summer **lightness**

AN UPHOLSTERED FOLDING SCREEN SERVES

MANY FUNCTIONS—AS AN INFORMAL BULLETIN

BOARD, A PARTIAL WINDOW TREATMENT, AND

AS A WORK OF ART.

See page 143 for fabric-covered panels.

indigo appeal

bright ideas
with cool color

In the color spectrum, blue is a cool color, making it an ideal choice for a summer bedroom. In addition, the combination of blue and white, so evocative of the sea and sky, is universally appealing. For a no-fail color scheme, mix intense and washed shades of the same blue. Add an abundance of white, along with a splash of warm yellow in the form of fresh flowers, a picture, or a lampshade for a light-creating accent.

Turn a bedroom into an airy retreat by pairing sheer drapes with a miscellany of blue cottons and denims for cushions and dust ruffle. Leave the floor and the rest of the furniture bare for a strong contrast. Make sure the windows are not obscured by heavy curtains—blue is a light-absorbing color, so leave the windows undressed or covered in sheers to brighten the room as much as possible.

SEAT CUSHIONS IN A MIX OF BLUES AND WHITES LEND COUNTRY CHARM TO AN ARRAY OF ANTIQUE CHAIRS. DON'T WORRY ABOUT MATCHED SETS—MIX AND MATCH SEATS AND CHAIRS FOR AN OFFBEAT, WHIMSICAL EFFECT.

See page 167 for tie-on cushions.

BLUE, ONE OF THE MOST TRANQUIL OF COLORS, BRINGS SERENITY TO A BEDROOM. TRANSPARENT BED CURTAINS OF VARYING WEIGHTS AND DESIGNS ARE COMPLEMENTED BY AN INDIGO BED COVER AND FRESH BLUE-AND-WHITE LINENS. THE CURTAINS ARE ATTACHED TO THE BED FRAME VIA BUTTONED LOOPS.

See pages 149 for unlined curtains, 150 for buttoned loops, and 155–7 for pillowcases.

summer **lightness**

Roman shades in a creamy linen blend into the background in this sitting room, allowing the wrought-iron settee to take center stage. The shades offer a veil of privacy, but when more light or view-blocking is needed, floor-to-ceiling draperies can be pulled.

See pages 165 for fitted box cushion, 160 for piped cushion edging, 147 for lined roman shades, and 149 for loose-lined curtains.

light reflections
windows that welcome the sun

Come summer, windows become especially important, as they link indoors and out. Capitalize on a window with a pleasant view or one that gets plenty of morning sun with a window seat amply padded with a cushion and pillows. Now it will offer a tantalizing view of the garden, while in winter it will become a favorite curling-up spot. If you don't have space for a small sofa, or preferably a built-in banquette, pull an armchair over to the window. To give meals an al fresco air, place a skirted table and chairs next to an open window for breakfast or even a dinner party.

With windows raised much of the time, opt for fabrics that move with breezes and gently diffuse the light. Dress your windows themselves in the airiest fabrics possible. If you love the look of sheers but need more privacy than they can offer, double up a sheer fabric, or team delicate shades or curtains with weightier draperies that can be pulled when necessary. If the view outside is the main attraction, choose fabrics that blend into the background—neutral-hued linens for roman shades, for example. Line them to make them completely opaque. Hard-working wood or metal blinds are a practical solution—they enable you to manipulate sunlight and air while still allowing fabric treatments to steal the show.

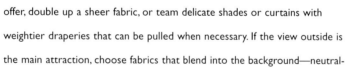

above

A NEATLY TAILORED ROMAN SHADE, LINED IN WHITE COTTON, FITS OVER A SHEER VOILE PANEL IN THIS WINDOW.

above right

PLENTIFUL BLUE-AND-WHITE PILLOWS BRING COMFORT TO AN IRON BENCH THAT WOULD BE EQUALLY AT HOME INDOORS OR OUT.

above

A GARDEN CHAIR GAINS THE COZINESS OF AN ARMCHAIR THANKS TO A SMOCK-LIKE COVER. POCKETS ON EITHER SIDE OF THE COVER CAN HOLD PAPERBACK BOOKS, SUNGLASSES, OR EVEN GARDENING GLOVES.

See pages 172–3 for tailored cover.

limelight

a burst of citrus
for a town house

Vivid citrus hues bring dazzle to rooms. High-voltage orange, tangy yellow, and zesty lime lend Caribbean warmth to any setting. Lime green in particular gives a modern glow—but do limit these shades to the public rooms of the house. In general, they are too strong for bedrooms, which usually need more restful hues.

For an unforgettable living room, decorate the whole space in shades of lime. Start with a contemporary chair upholstered in brilliant green linen and build your scheme around it. Continue the citrus theme throughout the room, but don't match all the shades exactly. Graduate from warm lemony green on the walls to sharp acid green for the furnishings and a mixture of muted greens and sherbet limes for the curtains. Take care matching the colors, however. Greens are amongst the trickiest colors to work with. Look for greens with a yellow base rather than a blue one. Greens with too much blue or black in them will clash with the lime colors. For the best effect, be sure to stick mainly with solid fabrics.

Such strong color needs to be tempered with whites or creams and a range of contrasting textures and weights. Mix delicate muslins with natural linen in different weights; team smooth cotton with shiny chintz and watch the room take shape.

Pale wooden floors have a calming effect on citrus shades, soaking up some of their impact. Rush matting or woven grass rugs or blinds will have a similar effect and offer a visual rest from the riot of color.

left, from the top

Such strong color needs bold accessories. A wrought-iron tieback is hefty enough to compete with the green draperies. Neutral rough linens for a loose chair cover and pillows help break up the color-dominated space. Cherrywood and gentle cream cotton and ceramics balance the acidity of the lime-green chairs.

See pages 173–4 for basket chair cover and 184 for rectangular tablecloth.

A RICH GREEN COTTON CURTAIN CONTRASTS
WITH A FILMY CHECKERED VOILE UNDERCURTAIN
THAT LETS IN THE LIGHT. THE OUTER DRAPERY
HAS A DEEPLY GATHERED HEADING, WHILE THE
INNER CURTAIN ATTACHES TO THE ROD WITH TIES.
**See pages 151 for gathered heading and
150 for tape ties on straight heading.**

zigzag finish **for a table cover**

Transform an ordinary round table (round plywood forms are sold in many catalogs) into a head-turning feature with an unusual skirt. Use a sturdy linen for the underskirt and top it with a lighter-weight piece of linen. A zigzag-edged cover for the topper adds a playful accent. Line the top layer so that it holds its shape; the lining will also ensure that the zigzags are well defined and do not fray. Sew little beads, tassels, or even bells onto the tips as eye-catching details. To make the most of the pattern, repeat it elsewhere. For example, use identical fabric to make a window valance with the same zigzag bottom. You could vary the design by using a scalloped edge instead.

materials

Main fabric, contrasting fabric, cotton lining fabric, 20 x ⅜" glass beads, thin
cardboard and pencil

measuring & cutting out *(fig 1)*

tablecloth

Top: cut a circle from main fabric, diameter = diameter of table top, plus 2". An
extra ⅜" is allowed all around for an easy fit.

Skirt: cut a rectangle from main fabric, length = circumference of fabric for top,
plus 9½", width = drop from table top to floor + 2⅛"

cover

Top: cut one circle from contrasting fabric, diameter = diameter of table top,
plus 2¼"

Edging: cut one rectangle from contrast fabric and one from lining,
length = length of skirt, plus 1½", width = 10". Ease is allowed for cover to fit
over cloth.

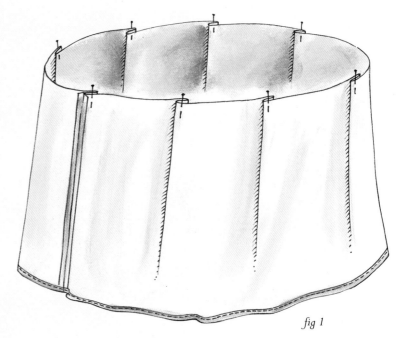

fig 1

making the tablecloth

1 With right sides together, join the two short edges of the skirt, making a ⅝"
seam. Turn up and stitch a ¾" double hem (equal turns) along the lower edge. Fold
in half from the seam, then into quarters and eighths. Mark each fold point with
pins. Starting at the seam, make a ⅝" pleat at each fold and pin in place *(fig 1)*.

2 Fold the circular top into half, then quarters, then eighths. Mark these folds
with pins at the outside edge and then, with right sides facing, pin the skirt
around the edge of the top, matching the pleats to the pins. Adjust the fullness of
the pleats as necessary. Check the fit on the table itself, then sew together,
making a ⅝" seam. Trim seam allowance to ⅜"

NB: To make a fuller fitted circular tablecloth in a finer fabric, the length of the
skirt must equal twice the circumference of the table.

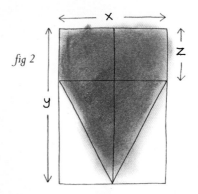

fig 2

making the cover

3 To work out how large each point should be, subtract 1¼" from the length of
the edging strip. Divide the remaining amount by 20 and cut out a rectangular
cardboard template which is this distance (x) wide and y (9") long. Draw a
horizontal line z (4") from the top and another which divides the rectangle in
half lengthwise. Draw a triangle in the lower half *(fig 2)* between these lines.

4 Starting ⅝" in from one short edge, and lining up the top with the upper edge
of the fabric, draw around the template onto the wrong side of the lining fabric
20 times to form a zigzag line. Leave ⅝" at the other end *(fig 3)*.

5 Sew into a loop with right sides together, with a ⅝" seam, and press flat. Join
the main fabric into a loop with right sides together, ⅝" from the ends. Press the
seam flat.

fig 3

6   With right sides together, pin the lining loop around the outside of the main fabric loop along the top and bottom edges. Baste close to the zigzag line *(fig 4)*, then stitch along it. Trim the surplus fabric, clip the corners (see p.139), and turn right side out. Pin and stitch the top edges together.

7   Pin and stitch the edging around the outside of the top with right sides together, making a ⅝" seam. Trim to ⅜" seam allowance. Stitch a glass bead securely to each point.

fig 4

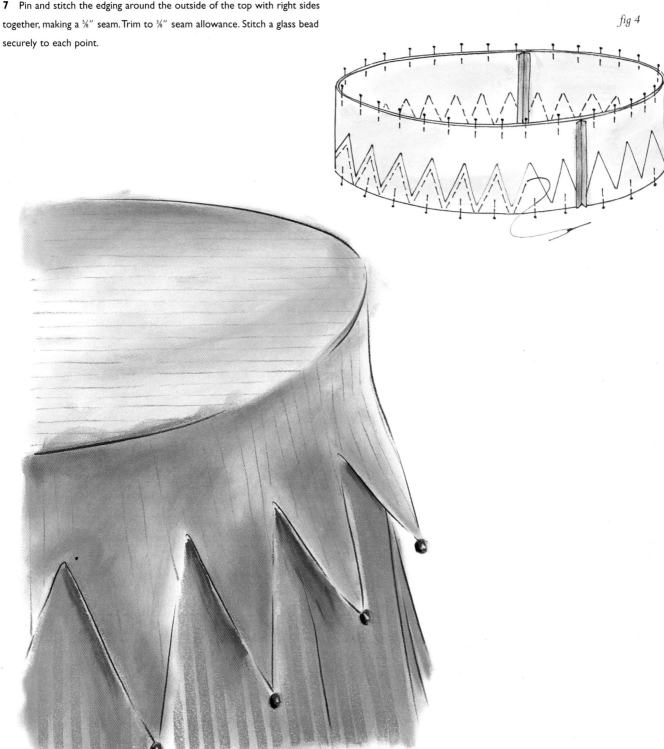

white havens

tranquility
for guest rooms

Swathe a guest bedroom in white cotton and linen to turn it into a restful sanctuary. White walls create a pristine enclosure—if pure white appears too strong, opt for porcelain and cream shades instead.

Decorating history has it that the French traditionally favored fabric for their walls, while the English preferred paper or paint. Follow the French for a true retreat. There are several ways to suspend wall hangings. You can either staple white cotton (sheets work well) to battens fixed to the wall, stretch wire or hang thin rods from one wall to another and thread the hemmed fabric over the wire, or you can secure the fabric at intervals to a Shaker-style pegboard with ties made from the same cotton. Cut out openings for windows, or if you wish to block the view entirely, let the fabric cover the windows. A few hints of color help break up the white expanse. The muted hues of old painted furniture add to the atmosphere. Or try a painted floor—simply tape out your design, paint, and then cover with several coats of polyurethane.

ROMANCE BY CANDLELIGHT—A
FOUR-POSTER BRASS BED IS DRESSED IN FINERY OF
CRISP COTTON, DELICATE LACE
AND TRANSLUCENT ORGANZA.

A PRETTY ORGANDY CURTAIN SCREENS OFF A

ROLL TOP BATH IN AN ENSUITE BATHROOM.

COOL COTTON AND LINEN PILLOWS ARE

CRISPLY STARCHED TO LOOK THEIR BEST.

73

permutations of white
for quiet luxury

White reflects light, making it an ideal choice for sticky summer days and nights. Despite its reputation, white can also be a practical option for interiors—preshrunk loose cotton slipcovers and tablecloths can be washed and dried quite easily.

Rather than dominating a room, a white sofa will introduce a sense of light, air and space, opening up the room by bringing in an air of freshness and a touch of abandon.

Continue the vacation mood with other shades. Deep blue-and-white cushion covers, patterned wallpaper and accessories mirror dappled summer skies and seas; textured creams and natural hues for window treatments and walls evoke sandy beaches. A bed covered in freshly laundered white linen is always an enticing sight. Buy fragments of antique linens to stitch together into an enchanting bedcover. Here's a hint: place and sew the pieces on a large cotton sheet to keep fragile edges from tearing and to simplify laundering and ironing.

left, above

A MULTITUDE OF BLUE-AND-WHITE FABRICS

BRIGHTEN AN OLD SLEIGH BED

left

A COLLECTION OF OLD LINEN AND LACE DOILIES,

PLACE MATS AND NAPKINS BECOMES A

MAGNIFICENT PATCHWORK BEDSPREAD.

A COMFORTABLE SOFA NEED NOT LOOK

BATTERED. MAKE A LOOSE COVER OUT OF WHITE

TEXTURED FABRIC THAT CAN BE WASHED. FINISH IT

WITH WELTING AND PLENTY OF PILLOWS.

See page 180 for slipcovers.

a country bedroom
with room for two

There are some specific ingredients in the recipe for an old-fashioned bucolic bedroom—bare wood floors, a pair of bedside tables, an iron bed and plenty of checked fabrics. Summer bedrooms, especially those for children, should be spare but not spartan—free of clutter and heavy furnishings.

When children have to double up in a summer bedroom, make the most of this decorating challenge by layering on the charm. The trick lies in letting the children express their individuality and giving each a semblance of privacy. For instance, old iron beds in different designs (allow them to choose their own if possible) and variations on the same red, white and black theme gives each child his or her own special space, but still gives the room a cohesive decorating scheme. Fabric screens come in handy in shared rooms—use them to carve out individual areas within the room. Practical considerations in children's rooms include washable rugs and shades or blinds at the window.

A LIGHTLY PADDED FABRIC SCREEN IS COVERED IN EMBROIDERED LINEN ON ONE SIDE, PLAIN LINEN ON THE OTHER.

See page 143 for fabric-covered panels.

left, above

A BURST OF ORANGE CHECKS AROUND THE SUN-SOAKED WINDOW LIGHTS UP THIS SIMPLE BEDROOM. WHITE WALLS SET THE COOL, CALM TONE OF THE REST OF THE SPACE. THE CURTAINS HAVE A FALL-BACK RUFFLE HEADING.

See page 152 for fall-back ruffle.

left

READING A SECRET BEDTIME STORY TAKES PRECEDENCE OVER SLEEP.

SIBLINGS AND COUSINS WILL LOVE A RUSTIC

DORMITORY, COMPLETE WITH MATCHING DUVETS

AND PILLOWCASES.

See pages 155–57 for pillowcases and

182 for quilt cover.

autumn
warmth

Despite what the calendar says, autumn is the natural beginning of the year, when life resumes its regularity after August's desultory days. Before the onset of winter, this is the last chance for football games, cookouts, long walks and other outdoor pleasures. By October, life has largely retreated indoors. Fabrics, like food, get heartier. Think of robust plaids, intricate paisleys, and woven fabrics that range from chevrons to tweeds. This return to interior living makes rooms that impart comfort and a welcoming air more important than ever—as we prepare to tuck ourselves in for the coming chill.

natural inspiration

Fall is a time of transition for the natural world as well as

our own. The greens of summer give way to the garnet

hues, tobacco browns and pumpkin colors of autumn. While

the garden fades, take a second look at the glorious foliage

of the season. Fill

pitchers with

sprays of dried

grasses, crystal

vases with

rhododendron leaves, or decorate rooms with pots of blazing

chrysanthemums. Woods take on extra import—uncover

cherry, mahogany or oak pieces and highlight their deep

hues with fabrics that echo them. Invest in an enveloping

throw of cashmere, heavy cotton or the finest wool and toss

it over a deep armchair for evenings by the fire. The point is

to immerse yourself in the season's fleeting joys.

new variations on
classic & contemporary

The colors and patterns of the autumnal tweeds and
plaids in this chapter take their cues from nature. These
classic fall fabrics have traditionally spoken of turning leaves,
silver seed heads, deep red berries and purple heather.
Today's fall hues, however, go beyond the deep
navys, burgundies and golds of the past—the
textiles of the season now come in very
unexpected colors. For example, old-fashioned
houndstooth is transformed by luminous green
and pink, or once-predictable plaids now come in
surprising combinations of jewel tones. Although fall
colors remain rich and warm, autumn is also about drama.
Think of the hills of northern Vermont ablaze with glory
on a late September day, and brighten your own fall
interiors with a few shots of bold color.

rough with the smooth
textures for contrast

Fall is the season of texture, when summer's smooth cottons give way to leathers, suedes, wools and tweeds. These comforting textures evoke fireside warmth. To make the most impact, however, textures need contrast. Team these rougher textiles with glossier yarns or fabrics with raised naps to draw attention to the assets of each. Mix pile fabrics in wild animal prints or glowing silks and damasks with more matte-finished wovens for interest.

Let the size of your room dictate the number of textures you use. A wide variety of textures will help visually shrink an overly large space, but for a small room confine yourself to no more than two textures to ensure a cohesive appearance in the space.

character study

contemporary pattern
for an old-fashioned room

Plaid, known as tartan in England, has a long and colorful history. As early as Roman times, Celtic people wore gaily colored plaids. This classic pattern—now in countless color permutations—continues to delight us today, especially in interiors.

Their reputation to the contrary, plaids do mix easily with other patterns. Team a plaid with an overscaled floral chintz for a charming room, or mix plaids with stripes or a simple two-color print such as a Napoleonic bee pattern. Be cautious combining different plaids—they can easily clash.

The key to combining plaids with other patterns is making sure the colors are the same. Solid shades that draw out the colors in the plaid are always enchanting. In this room, the ruby color of the table's underskirt is echoed in an overskirt, while the blue of the plaid is repeated in the walls.

left

A WELL-WORN ARMCHAIR GAINS NEW STYLE FROM A CONTEMPORARY PLAID SLIPCOVER. UNLIKE THE LOOSE SLIPCOVERS OF SUMMER, WOOL OR COTTON PLAID SLIPCOVERS LOOK BEST WHEN TAILORED.
See pages 178–80 for slipcovers for armchairs and 160 for piped pillow.

right

THE TOP AND SIDES OF THIS JEWEL-HUED TABLE SKIRT ARE SEWN SEPARATELY, THEN STITCHED TOGETHER SO THAT THE BOTTOM SKIRT FALLS IN GENEROUS FOLDS. TO MAKE THIS TOP COVER, ADAPT THE INSTRUCTIONS FOR THE ZIGZAG TABLE COVER **(see pages 70–1).**

cozy nights **under a lined duvet**

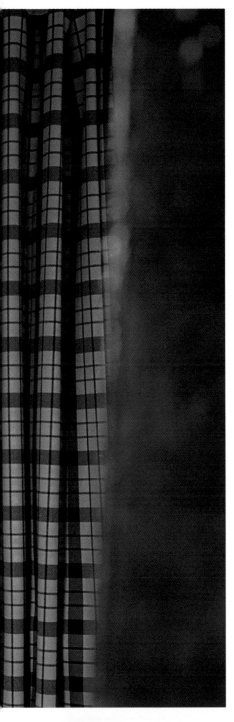

The crisp nights of fall make delightful sleeping weather. This bed's plump duvet and enveloping curtains ward off any frosty drafts. The curtains are constructed essentially as large fabric bags (see page 143) that attach to the frame via buttoned loops.

The check/plaid combination of the bed-curtains marries easily with the plaid duvet cover, thanks to the fact that the curtains are only two colors, which keeps the fabrics from clashing.

An ivory linen sheet ensures that the underside of the wool duvet cover stays soft against a sleeper's skin. It attaches to the cover with buttons at the top and bottom.

materials

Main fabric for quilt cover, linen or cotton sheeting, red embroidery thread, 18 ¾" buttons

measuring & cutting out (see fig 1)

Join widths as necessary, with a flat fell seam (see p.139)

quilt cover

Cut two: width = a + 3¼", depth = b + 5⅜"

sheet

Cut one: width = a + 7", length = b + 48"

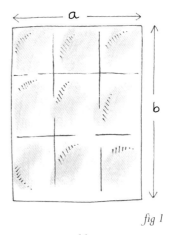

fig 1

assembling

1 Pin the front and back of the quilt cover with right sides together, and stitch around the two long and one short edge, making a ⅜" seam. Trim the seam allowance and finish with a zigzag.

2 Press under ⅜" around the open end, then turn under a further 2⅜". Stitch down close to the fold and press. Make six evenly spaced buttonholes along the front, ¾" from the edge, by hand or machine. Sew six buttons to the inside of the back edge in the corresponding positions to close.

3 Sew a row of six evenly spaced buttons to the top and six to the bottom of the front, 20" from the edge.

4 Make a 1¼" double hem (equal turns) around all four edges of the sheet, mitering the corners (see p.140) if desired. Make six buttonholes by hand or machine along the double border at each short end to match the buttons on the comforter. Put the quilt inside the cover. Then with the sheet centered under the quilt, fold the sheet ends over the quilt and button the ends of the sheet in place.

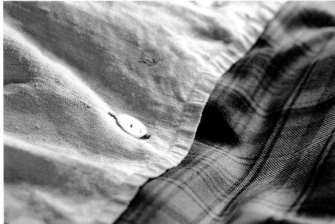

a plethora of plaid

formal & *informal*
from castle to cottage

One of the joys of plaid lies in its flexibility—it can easily hold its own against either the rustic or the grand, looking equally at home in a chic apartment or a country farmhouse. The tartan plaids are timeless and convey tradition, while more innovative color combinations invoke a modern spirit. For the most impact, mix classic and unusual plaids, or reverse the expected and put small plaids on large wing chairs or sofas, and large plaids on small pillows or dainty side chairs.

In this cottage-style bedroom, fresh blue-and-white sheets set the country theme, while a box-pleated plaid dust ruffle offsets the cuteness of the mini-checks. A playful touch: the interior of the box pleats is the familiar Royal Stewart tartan. Tie this additional plaid into the rest of the room scheme by echoing it in other subtle touches—in a throw over a bedside chair, a dressing-table skirt, or in a window valance. Let the fabrics claim the stage by keeping the walls and floors natural hues.

FLASHES OF ROYAL STEWART TARTAN IN THE CORNERS OF THE BOX-PLEATED DUST RUFFLE SET OFF THE BLUE-AND-WHITE CHECKS OF THE FITTED SHEET.

See page 183 for box-pleated dust ruffle.

left

A PLAID CUSHION BECKONS WELCOME TO A
FAVORITE WINDOW SEAT.
See page 165 for fitted box cushion.

below

SMALL BUT PRACTICAL, FOOTSTOOLS PROVIDE
MUCH COMFORT CONSIDERING THEIR SIZE. SNAP
UP OLD ONES AT ANTIQUE STORES OR FLEA
MARKETS AND COVER THEM WITH A DOUBLE-
FLOUNCED TOPPER MADE FROM PLAID REMNANTS.
TO STITCH THIS COVER, ADAPT THE PLAID TABLE
SKIRT **(see pages 104–5)**.

WHERE WOULD TAILGATE PARTIES OR SEPTEMBER PICNICS BE WITHOUT WARM PLAID BLANKETS TO LAY ON

THE GROUND OR WRAP UP IN? FOR THIS FALL OUTING, AN INEXPENSIVE DIRECTOR'S CHAIR HAS THE

WARMTH OF A FIRESIDE ARMCHAIR THANKS TO A PLAID SLIPCOVER.

oasis in the heather
for an autumn outing

A thick plaid blanket spread out in the midst of an apple orchard or even on a still-green field in the center of a city park provides an oasis on a leaf-looking excursion. It is the perfect setting for an outdoor feast of thick soup and nutty bread, with picnickers swathed in layers of wool and furry throws. Wool blankets, fringed, tasseled or plain, make a perfect base for such an outing, or an early-morning stroll or an afternoon blackberry hunt. This is why the use of plaid inside a house can be so effective in creating a country atmosphere—it immediately conjures up images of a hearty outdoor life.

These blankets provide many functions—as picnic ground covers, or as sofa or bed throws. Beautiful to look at, wool, mohair or cashmere blankets are the epitome of warmth and comfort. The power of plaid to warm the everyday can be seen in this chair cover for a run-of-the-mill director's chair. Dressed in a lively heather-hued frock, it becomes an inviting seat. Although not as expected as typical fall reds and golds, heather is a typical English fall hue. When searching for just the right heather plaid, don't settle for a watered-down version of the real thing. To match it exactly, take a bunch of real heather along to the fabric shop, and pick a plaid, check or tweed that does justice to that vivid purple.

THE FABRIC COVER ON THIS CHAIR HAS BEEN CAREFULLY CUT AND SEWN SO THAT THE LINES OF THE PLAID MATCH ACROSS THE CHAIR. THIS IS THE TRICKY PART OF SEWING WITH PLAIDS—THE LINES MUST MEET EXACTLY ALONG SEAMS AND CORNERS OR THE WHOLE COVER WILL APPEAR CARELESS.
See pages 174–5 for director's chair cover.

decorative touches
remnants convey personal style

A FLANNEL THROW GAINS EXTRA SOFTNESS

FROM A FUN-FUR BACKING.

See page 182 for throws.

Be inventive with your fabric remnants by sewing one-of-a-kind accessories that give your rooms cohesiveness and your home true personality. The ideas are endless. You could stitch up place mats, napkins, curtain tiebacks, a trimming for a lampshade, a lining for a log holder or a picnic basket from extra scraps. Or, mix and match different plaids for a patchwork effect. Deep royal purple mixed with forest green makes a particularly rich plaid. Here, it is used for picnic cutlery rolls, tied with a left-over length of fabric or a plaid ribbon. When not being used for picnics, you could also use these rolls as clever place mats.

If your leftovers aren't quite enough to accomplish your project, use this opportunity to add another texture to the mix. Wool plaids look especially inviting when backed with thickly piled fur-like synthetics.

opposite

A CUTLERY ROLL IN DEEP PURPLE AND FOREST

GREEN PLAID IS A HANDY EXTRA ON A PICNIC,

YET IS SMART ENOUGH FOR A DINNER-PARTY

PLACE MAT. DRESS IT UP WITH YOUR

SUNDAY-BEST SILVERWARE.

See page 185 for flatware roll.

modern eccentrics

trendy tweeds
go uptown

Just as a tweed blazer on a person implies a bookish, traditional nature, so do tweed soft furnishings convey similar characteristics in a room. But tweed need not appear fusty; when contrasted with sleek vibrant fabrics, old-fashioned herringbone and houndstooth weaves take on a new persona. A word of advice: tailoring is as important with tweed furnishings as it is with a tweed outfit. The cover must sit well on the shape of the sofa or chair and careful attention must be paid to details such as buttons, piping and fringing.

In this high-style apartment, traditional herringbone tweed appears on the curtains and its colors are picked up in a more modern weave on an armchair. The traditional sofa is swathed in a dark-gray velvet cover updated with throws and pillows in exotic colors. Dressmaker details such as button and fringe update tweed cushions. The curtains are fringed as well, and gathered onto a header tape. The curtains have been left unlined to allow the light to filter through the weave. But these draperies could easily be lined with a contrasting fabric or a solid lining to block the light and provide additional protection from drafts.

above & detail right

Herringbone suiting material creates unusual but handsome curtains. The naturally fraying edges make charming fringe when gathered onto a header tape. The armchair repeats the colors of the curtains in a bolder tweed pattern.

See pages 151 for buttoned-pleat curtain heading and 178–80 for slipcovers for armchairs.

above

A TWEED-COVERED SOFA GOES MODERN

THANKS TO VIBRANT THROWS AND PILLOWS

IN SOLID COLORS.

See pages 182 for throws and 158–60

for pillows.

left

THESE EASY-TO-SEW PILLOWS ARE FRINGED AND

BUTTONED TO MATCH THE CURTAINS.

red, white & blue
with a twist

When it comes to decorating nurseries, most new parents overdo on cuteness, and the next thing they know, they are faced with redecorating. Instead, choose classic colors and patterns to create a room that will grow with your child. Remember as well that strong contrasting colors have instant appeal for babies and small children, and all-American red, white and blue is one of the best-loved color combinations there is. In this toddler's bedroom, creamy yellow walls set the stage and keep attention focused on the lively mix of plaids and checks.

A subtle navy-and-cream plaid forms the crib bumper, which accents the azure-and-white linen coverlet. A pure white linen sheet attaches to the coverlet with ties for softness against the baby's skin. Both sheet and coverlet can be removed for easy washing.

Deeply zigzagged valances decorated with pompons bring a whimsical touch to the long windows. They top plain linen blinds, which can be pulled down at night. Red plaid window-seat cushions echo the window fabric and provide a home for teddy bears and dolls.

top

DETAIL OF THE CHAIR COVER TIED WITH BOWS AT

THE BACK.

above

COLORFUL POMPONS HIGHLIGHT THE ZIGZAG

EDGE OF A WINDOW VALANCE. A LINEN ROMAN

SHADE HANGS BEHIND IT, READY TO BE LOWERED

AT NIGHTTIME.

See pages 152 for valances and 146 for

soft roman shade.

left

A CHEERFUL RED PLAID COVER THAT TIES AT THE

BACK ENLIVENS AN ORDINARY WOODEN CHAIR.

See pages 172–3 for tailored cover and 165

for fitted box cushion.

opposite & detail left

THIS CRIB FEATURES AN EMBROIDERED WHITE

COTTON OVER-SHEET THAT TIES BACK TO PROTECT

THE COVERLET; IT ALSO CREATES A SOFTER, MORE

DECORATIVE EDGE. ZIGZAGS BECOME A

RECURRING THEME AROUND THE ROOM.

DIFFERENT SKIRTS IN THE SAME RED PLAID

FABRIC GIVE DISTINCTION TO A PAIR OF

ANTIQUE MAHOGANY CHAIRS. THE RICHNESS

OF PLAID GOES WELL WITH DARK WOODS

AND GOTHIC-STYLE FURNISHINGS.

See page 169 for box-pleated seat cover.

SAVE ON REUPHOLSTERING BY GIVING WORN

CHAIRS NEW SLIPCOVERS. THE LINES OF THIS

BEDROOM CHAIR ARE EMPHASIZED BY A SLIPCOVER

SEWN FROM A TIGHTLY WOVEN WOOL PLAID.

See pages 176–7 for bedroom chair cover.

chair lifts
re-covering in red

Nothing brightens a room like a strong dash of red. A bold red tape on a dark wooden blind adds dash to a formal study. The color jolt of a red pillow softens the formality of a pristine white chair. Red comes in many forms—oxblood, scarlet, cherry—each has its own appeal. Remember, red is never shy; it demands attention. Make the most of red's look-at-me properties to either accentuate an unusual piece or enliven an ordinary one. Slipcovers for chairs, settees and sofas are a pragmatic choice if you fear you may tire of your red room after you've lived with it awhile.

below

THIS SHAPELY PAINTED SETTEE BECOMES EVEN MORE EYE-CATCHING WHEN COVERED WITH A RED PLAID CUSHION AND A LIVELY MIX OF PILLOWS. See pages 185 for fitted box cushion, 141 for decorative cord edgings, and 162–3 for gathered end bolsters.

To ensure that your chair covers fit properly, make up a mock cover first, using an old sheet, then use t hat as a template for the real thing. Loose covers are especially practical for lighter colors and fine fabrics, as they can be removed and cleaned readily. If you prefer more upholstered-looking pieces, just be sure the cover fits as snugly as possible, with little room for movement. You can accomplish this by making the cover as you would a tailored suit. Sew darts where necessary and employ Velcro fastenings to attach the cover tightly to the frame.

The potential for re-covering tired furniture is limitless. Wrap the seat of an old chaise in new plaid and pile it with mismatched pillows. Cheer up a somber hall chair by tying on a seat cushion with a flouncy skirt. Always add skirts or frills last of all to your slipcovers—experiment with length and shape until the proportions are right for your piece. Follow the rules of fashion and keep skirts short for attractive, well-carved legs, full length for chunky ones.

plaid cover **for a dressing table & stool**

Continuity in a home is crucial. Colors should flow from one room to the next for a harmonious feel. To give a master bedroom and bath an ensuite air, use the same fabrics in each. In this case, the fabric of the chair covering in the bedroom is restated in the covers for a dressing room table and stool. This link is all it takes to unify these two rooms. Color cues can come from anywhere—echo the hues in the bedroom rug or the curtains in the bathroom. Remember, however, that bathroom slipcovers should always be loose so that they can be removed and cleaned with ease.

materials

Main fabric, contrasting fabric, piping cord (length = a + 2c + 6″)

measuring & cutting out *(figs 1 & 2)*

Make a paper template to fit the top of both table and stool, following the method shown on p.166. Add an extra ⅜″ all around for an easy fit. For a dresser that has an in-built mirror, cut the ruffle and skirt in two pieces and leave two gaps to fit around the struts. Lengths "a" and "c" refer to the enlarged template pieces.

table

Top: cut one as template from contrasting fabric, plus 1″ all around

Ruffle: cut one from contrasting fabric, width = z (8¾″), length = 1½a

Skirt: cut one from main fabric, width = b + 2″, length = 2a

making the table cover

1 Cut a length of piping cord, measuring a + 2″, and cover it with a bias strip of the main fabric. Pin the covered cord to the right side of the top ½″ from edge. Clip the curves and join the edges (see p.141). Stitch in place with a zipper foot.

2 Pin the ruffle into a loop with right sides together, and stitch ⅝″ from the short edges. Press the seam flat. Zigzag one long edge of the ruffle, then turn up and stitch a ¾″ single hem. With right sides together and matching the raw edges, pin around the edge of the top, making ⅜″ pleats at 2″ intervals *(fig 3)*. (Divide the circumference by eight, then follow the technique for attaching a ruffle to a rectangle on p.142 to make sure that the fullness is distributed evenly). Adjust the pleats as necessary, so they look even. Stitch in place ½″ from the edge, using a zipper foot.

3 Zigzag the short edges of the skirt and turn under a ¾″ single hem, then do the same along the lower edge. With right sides together, pin the two unhemmed corners to the center front of the top. Pin the right side of the skirt around the edge to the wrong side of the ruffle, making 1¼″ pleats approximately every 2¾″. Put the cover over the table to check the fit, then stitch through all the layers, close to the piping. Press.

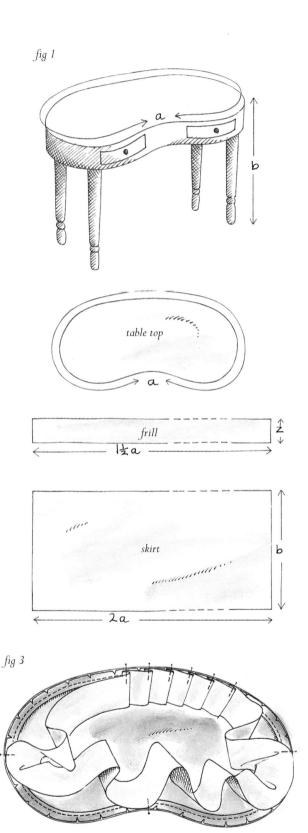

fig 1

table top

a

frill

1½a

skirt

b

2a

fig 3

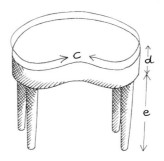

stool *(fig 4)*

Top: cut one as template from main fabric, plus ⅝″ all around

Collar: cut one from main fabric, width = d + 1¼″, length = c + 1¼″

Ruffle: cut one from main fabric, width (y) = 8″, length = 1½c + 1¼″

Skirt: cut one from contrasting fabric, width = e + 1½″, length = 2c + 2″

making the stool cover

1 Cover the remaining piping cord with contrasting fabric and cut in two. Sew one length to the right side of the stool top, joining the ends neatly. Pin the two short ends of collar with right sides together and stitch, ⅝″ from the edge. Press the seam open, then sew the second length of piping to the right side of lower edge. Pin the top edge to the stool top and check the fit before stitching *(fig 5)*.

2 Sew the ruffle and skirt into loops along their short edges. Turn up ¾″ double hems (equal turns) at the lower edges. Pin the ruffle to the collar along the piping with right sides together, distributing the fullness evenly. Make a series of ¾″ pleats, 3⅛″ apart. Pin the skirt to the ruffle, as in step 3 opposite, making a 1″ pleat every 2″. Stitch through all the layers, and press.

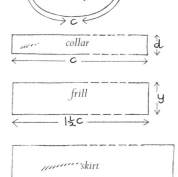

fig 4

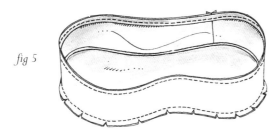

fig 5

winter

glow

If ever a season seemed to call out for decorating, it is winter. And not only because the holidays offer an irresistible excuse to revel in a love of design. Winter itself invites decorating ingenuity. As the outdoor scene becomes forbidding, home becomes our sanctuary—our buffer against bitter winds and gloomy days.

Swathe rooms in layers of soothing fabrics; add shimmery touches that capture and reflect every fragment of light. Kindle a fire. And take comfort in the words of 19th-century poet John Greenleaf Whittier: "The Night Is Mother of the Day, the Winter of the Spring."

natural inspiration

When it comes to cold-weather decorating, there are two schools of thought. One technique counteracts the world beyond the window; the other makes the most of it. Each has its own beauty. For the first, fill rooms with saturated hues of hearty reds, greens and golds, and wrap windows and furniture in enfolding fabrics such as velvet or damask. For the second, borrow from the Scandinavians, who know well how to make the most of winter's faint light. They seed their spaces with mirrors, silver and crystal, and paint their walls and furniture the colors of snow.

rich & sophisticated
for dramatic effects

Much of the inspiration for the fabric in this chapter comes from
the street markets of Asia, where dazzling-hued fabrics are ubiquitous.
Not for the fainthearted, these textiles are unabashedly exotic,
resplendent with color and detail. They should be put together with the
same joyful abandon with which you might decorate a Christmas tree.
We have taken gold and scarlet, silver, bronze and caramel creams,
and teamed them with brilliant greens, blues, vibrant pinks and
deep purples. Patterns—stripes, paisleys and embroidered
florals—are as dramatic as the colors and highly
intricate. Their details are a feast for the eyes.

soft & luxurious
textures for contrast

If summer is the casual season—a time of shorts and bathing suits—then winter is the time of elegance—of satin and velvet gowns. Nothing imparts a sense of luxury more easily than fabrics. Consider the feel of your materials, their sheen, heft, and overall beauty—the classics are still unbeatable: silk, velvet, damask, and crisp taffeta. And just as presents are always much more enticing when wrapped with a flourish of ribbons, so do these fabrics become even more luxurious when embellished with such details as tassels, fringe and braid. Remember as well to be generous with the amount of fabric. The deeper the pleats, the tighter the ruching, the longer the drape, the more elaborate the look.

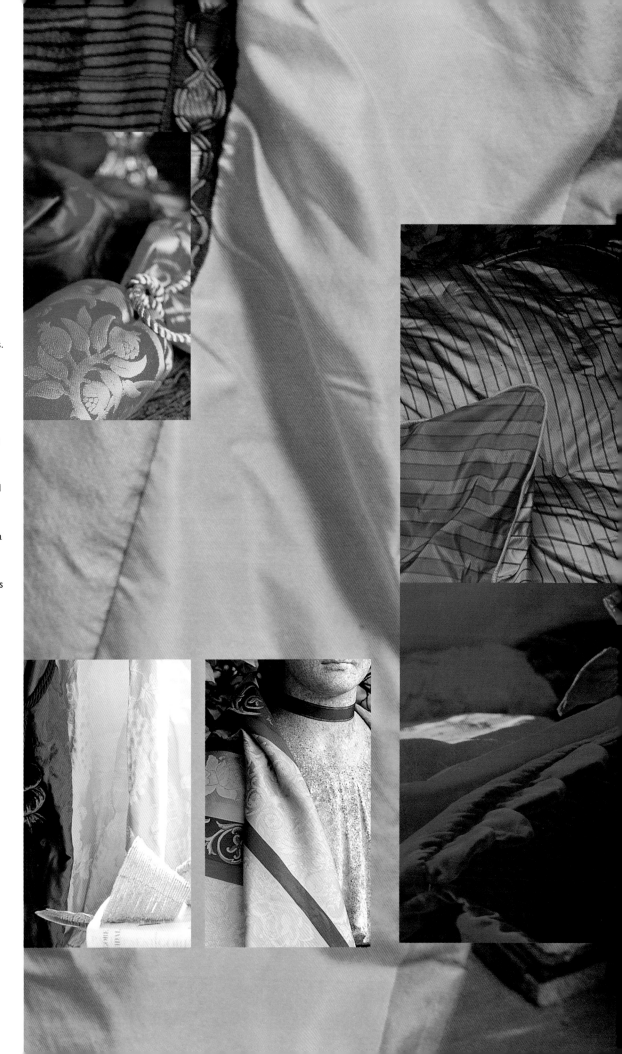

winter fantasy

shimmery & sophisticated
furniture dressed to celebrate

When it comes to decorating, the Scandinavians do not hide from winter—they delight in it. They make their homes as airy and as quietly glittering as the world outside. Even if there's not a snowflake in sight, you can turn your home into a romantic vision of an interior snowscape. Layer on shimmering taffetas, silks and organzas, or gold or silver-threaded translucent fabrics that reflect and enhance all light—whether it be sunshine or the glow of candles. Maximize the sparkle with mirrors, as well as silver and gold, glass and crystal accessories. And don't forget the candlelight. Remember, however, to keep walls pale to reflect as much light as possible.

Glimmering fabrics do give rooms a formal air—making them perfect for holiday decorating. Silver and gold materials in particular impart a festive atmosphere. This silver silk table skirt was actually sewn from (and inspired by) a drop-waisted ball gown. You can trace its ancestry in the deep pleats, the pointed overcloth, and the floor-gracing folds of fabric.

right

A SILVER SILK BALL GOWN IS REBORN AS A DRAMATIC TABLE SKIRT TOPPED WITH AN ORGANDY OVERCLOTH EDGED WITH TINY GRAY PEARLS. THE GATHERED CIRCULAR TABLECLOTH IS A FULLER VERSION OF THE ZIGZAG FINISH TABLECOVER **(see pages 68–69)**.

An antique iron cradle becomes a work of
art when draped in gauzy fabrics as delicate
as a sari, along with richly woven brocades.
The curtains in the room (see opposite,
also) are layers of orange muslin and
yellow embroidered chiffon.
See page 149 for unlined curtains.

sheer delights
two bedrooms transformed

The beauty of diaphanous fabrics lies in their ability to diffuse light. When tinged in zingy colors they turn pale winter sunlight into a rainbow glow. These two bedrooms amply illustrate the magical qualities of colored sheers. In one bedroom, brilliantly hued sheer fabrics and intricately woven brocades found in every market stall in India—and ethnic boutiques here—make over an antique wrought-iron crib into a dream from *The Arabian Nights*. The curtains are made from orange-dyed muslin with an over-curtain of yellow embroidered chiffon, which contrast sharply with the pink-and-lilac canopy on the crib. The effect is one of multicolored warmth, and just these two fabric creations—the canopy and the curtains—create the illusion of a glowing Indian sunset. The rest of the room is relatively bare, with wooden floors, pale washed walls and gilded curtain tiebacks.

In the other bedroom, a multitude of ethnic fabrics make a four-poster daybed into a setting worthy of a sheik. The yellow walls are a reminder of sunny days, while the colorful kilims on the floors call to mind another world.

right

SUN STREAMS THROUGH LONG WINDOWS,

ILLUMINATING THE GAUZY SILKS AND CHIFFONS

DRAPED ACROSS THE EASTERN FOUR-POSTER BED.

A DAYROOM IN FRENCH EMPIRE STYLE IS DECORATED IN PALE GRAYS, LILAC, BLUES AND WHITE. THE

FABRICS ARE NEW AND OLD DAMASKS AND BROCADES.

See pages 170–1 for flounced cover skirt and 158–60 for pillows.

crisp & even
serenity in a wintry rooms

In most northern climes, winter is remarkable for its absence of color. Silvers, grays, whites, and creams typify wintry landscapes in many areas. There is a calming beauty in these neutral hues that translates easily into a soothing design scheme. In the dayroom, the upright chairs wear gray silk frocks trimmed in gold brocade, details of which are shown below. The daybed is covered in white ribbed fabric with gray piping, as is the armchair; but a soft ivory velvet or moire would have worked equally well. An overscaled gilt-framed, crackle-glazed mirror reflects the light and is one of the room's few ornaments. When searching for furnishings, do not overlook stone or painted wood pieces, which possess the appropriate patina for such an ethereal space.

In such a pale setting one bold dash of color—in the form of a rug, a painting or even a pillow—makes a strong impact.

A HINT OF PALE BLUE IN A PAINTED TABLE ADDS A GENTLE TOUCH OF COLOR TO A SERENE ROOM. THE COTTON GRAY-AND-WHITE CURTAINS ARE A SOFT AND FRIENDLY COUNTERPOINT TO THE FORMAL SILK CHAIRS.

right

A SNOWY LANDSCAPE IS TRANSLATED INTO GRAY SILK FABRIC FOR THE CHAIRS AND CHAISE LONGUE.

See pages 171 for pleated chair cover and 161 for bolsters.

sensuous silk **for a luxurious quilt**

Despite its delicate appearance, silk is a warm fabric, making it ideal for a winter quilt. And today's abundance of washable and synthetic silks make it as practical and inexpensive as cotton. Silk takes dyes beautifully and can hold deep rich colors and bold designs that tend to fade in cotton. The stripes of this red-and-ochre quilt enhance the beauty of the fabric itself.

materials

Main fabric for the top, contrasting fabric for the back, length of covered piping = 2a +2b, plus 2″, chalk pencil, strong thread, 12 x 1¼″ self-cover buttons

measuring & cutting (see fig 1)

Cut top and back alike: width (a) = width of quilt, length (b) = length of quilt, plus ⅝″ all around.
Cut 12 circles from each fabric using the template supplied with the buttons.

assembling

1   Mark three points on the right side along each long edge of both pieces (about ¼ the width in from the edge); two 15¾″ from the corners and the third halfway between them. Matching raw edges, pin the piping to the right side of the back. Curve it gently at the corners and join the ends (see p.141). Stitch, using a zipper foot *(fig 1)*.

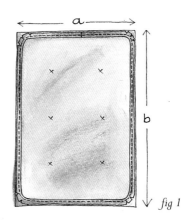

fig 1

2   With right sides together, pin the top to the back. Sew together just inside the previous stitch line, close to the cord, and leave a 3′ opening along one short edge. Fold back and press unstitched seam allowance on the front. Clip corners, turn right side out, and press. Insert the comforter and slipstitch the opening.

3   Make up the buttons according to the instructions and thread a long needle with a double length of button thread. Thread the needle through the shank of the first button and tie it on securely, 4″ from the knot. Push the needle through the quilt at the first mark and out the other side at the corresponding point. Thread it through the shank of the second button and take it back to the right side *(fig 2)*. Stitch through the quilt again once or twice, then knot the thread tightly and clip the ends. Repeat for the other buttons.

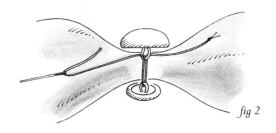

fig 2

carnival of color

blending cultures
for a festive fête

Parties held in the dark depths of winter should be as bright and colorful as possible. Imbue your house with a carnival atmosphere using a collection of jewel-like fabrics in exotic colors and textures. This merry gathering gains its theatrical air from the combination of Renaissance and Eastern elements.

The table for this fancy-dress party is resplendent in gold, blue and red. A mixture of fabrics adorns the table—a striped damask and a fine paisley trimmed at the corners with silken tassels. The gold-painted chairs are dressed in silken seat covers, which tie on with silver bows. An abundance of candles enhances the party atmosphere.

above & right

JEWEL-LIKE FABRICS BRIGHTEN A TABLE FOR A

MIDWINTER PARTY.

all the trimmings
chairs that charm

In Medieval times chairs were a luxury, reserved for the owner of the manor and honored guests. But by the end of the 16th-century in Great Britain and Europe, chairs had become relatively commonplace, especially in larger country estates. Chairs became an important element in the art of conversation. Dress up your "conversation chairs" with rich brocades and taffetas to rival the mansions of the past. Raid fabric and trimmings stores for dressmaker details such as fringe and ribbons to adorn your favorite chairs. In this living room, a length of striped silk revitalizes a sofa; silk pillows edged in gold fringe and tied with green ribbons complete the updated look. A velvet armchair is piled with soft velvet pillows in crimson and green, while a stool is made into a small masterpiece with a crimson damask slipcover. Make sure the rest of the room lives up to this opulence by adding fabric wall coverings, decorative screens and lampshades and clusters of glittering accents.

PLEATED TAFFETA RIBBON TRIMS A WOVEN PAISLEY THROW. THE PLEATED LAMPSHADE FEATURES A GATHERED SILK RIBBON ALONG THE EDGE.
See page 154 for ruffled lampshade.

left

A STRIPED SILK THROW COVERS A SOFA THAT NEEDS BRIGHTENING. FAT BOLSTERS TIED WITH GREEN RIBBON ADD COMFORT.
See pages 182 for throws and 158–60 for pillows.

right

A DIRECTOR'S CHAIR MAKES PERFECT OCCASIONAL SEATING WHEN DRESSED IN A GORGEOUS SLIPCOVER.
See page 176 for director's chair with hood.

far right

A SKIRTED DAMASK STOOL COVER IS GATHERED UP AT THE FOUR CORNERS TO REVEAL GILDED LEGS.
See page 181 for ruched cover footstool.

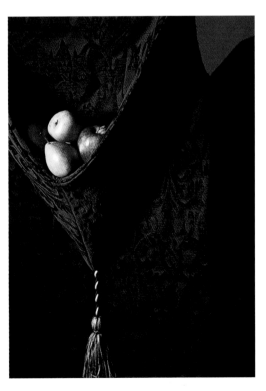

couture dressing **for baby baskets**

Create Moses baskets with deep reds and soft fabrics—cuddly comforts that babies won't want to grow out of. These baskets are lined in various red-hued velvets and silks—the color is strong and reassuring to a baby, and the feel of the fabrics suitably gentle.

Don't limit these versatile and beautiful baskets to babies, however. They can be used to show off dolls or teddy bears, or to hold needlepoint or sewing materials. The linings detach easily for cleaning. Make plain or quilted coverlets in the same fabric. Add pretty scalloped and frilled edging and trim with silk and velvet ribbons.

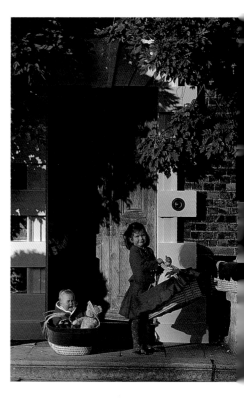

materials

Baby basket, paper and pencil, main fabric, contrasting fabric (for quilt only), batting

measuring & cutting out the basic basket liner (figs 1 & 2)

Make the base template by placing the basket on a sheet of paper and drawing around it. The template should be approximately ⅝″ larger all around than the inside. To make the quilt pattern, cut 8″ off the head end and add an extra 1″ around the remaining edges.

For the sides, cut a long strip of paper, length "a" and the same width as the highest point of the basket, "c". Tape it around the basket and cut the top edge to match the curve. Split it at the center of each side to make separate patterns for the head and foot sections, adding ⅝″ all around; for ruffled and scalloped edges, add an extra 1″ along the top edges.

lining

Head section: cut one as template. Notch the center bottom edge.

Foot section: cut one as template. Notch the center bottom edge.

Base: cut one as template. Notch the center sides, and head and foot.

Plain edge: cut two 3¼″ strips of fabric to fit around the head and foot, using the upper edge of the lining templates (indicated by line "g") as a guide.

Ruffle: cut four 6″-wide strips; 1 = 2e, 1 = 2f, and 2 = 2d

Ties: cut four strips: width = 5″, length = 20″

Scallops: cut three 6″-wide strips of paper to fit around the head and foot, using the upper edge of the lining templates (indicated by line "h") as a guide.

The length of these strips should correspond to lines "d," "e," and "f," so that the scallops will fit around the handles. Mark the cutting line for scallops as shown on the pattern *(fig 2)* and add ⅝″ all around each piece.

Cut two foot pieces, two heads, and four sides.

assembling

1 Join the two side lining pieces (head and foot) together at the short edges, with right sides facing, making a ⅝″ seam. For a ruffled or scalloped edge, press under ⅜″ along the top edge; topstitch. Pin the lower edge to the base with right sides together. Match the notches at the center head and foot, and align the side seams with the side notches on the base. Continue pinning, making two small pleats on each side of the head to take in the surplus fabric, and another two at the foot as necessary *(fig 3)*. Stitch, ⅝″ from the edge.

for a plain edge

2 Sew the two strips together along the short ends with right sides facing to form a loop, then press the seams flat. Make a ⅜″ double hem along the lower edge. Pin and stitch the strip to the top of the lining, with right sides together, matching the seams. This will form a tight, narrow band that will hold the lining in place around the top edge and fit behind the handles.

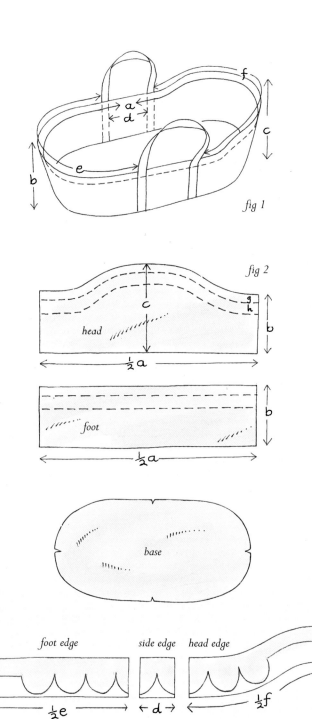

fig 1

fig 2

head ½a b

foot ½a b

base

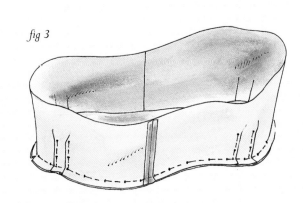

foot edge   side edge   head edge

½e   ←d→   ½f

fig 3

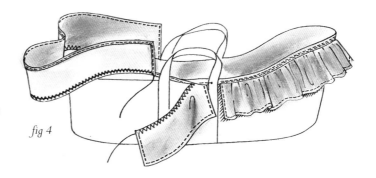

for a ruffled edge

2   The ruffle is made in four parts, so that it can fit around the handles. Make a narrow double hem along the short and lower edges of each piece. Notch the center top edge of the two longer pieces. Sew a zigzag gathering thread (see p.142) along the raw edges.

3   Place the lining, right side up, inside the basket. Pin the raw edges of the ruffles in place at head, foot, and sides. Attach them with right sides facing to the underside of the finished edge of the liner, matching the notches at head and foot *(fig 4)*.

4   Remove the lining from the basket and pull up the gathering threads to fit. Adjust the fullness so that it lies evenly and stitch down, over the threads. Trim the ruffle seam allowance to ¼", then turn over ⅝" all around the top edge to cover the raw edges. Topstitch.

5   Make the ties as on p.144. Fold in half, then sew two to each sides at the handle spaces. Place the finished lining in the basket and tie in place.

for a scalloped edge

6   With right sides together, pin the pieces together in pairs and stitch the scallop lines around the sides and lower edge of each. Trim, clip the curves (see p.139), and turn right side out. Pin the four sections to the turned-back seam allowance of the basket, as for the ruffled edge, stitch in place, and trim the seam allowance to ¼". Turn over a further ⅝" and topstitch.

quilt *(fig 5)*

Top: cut one from main fabric

Back: cut one from contrasting fabric

Border: cut one, width (x) = 7", length = width of top

Batting: cut one, ⅜" smaller all around than the template

making the quilt

7   Turn under a ⅜" single hem along one long side of the border. With right sides together, pin the raw edge to the top edge of the quilt top and stitch, ⅜" from the edge.

8   Baste the batting to the wrong side of the back. With the border sandwiched between the two layers *(fig 6)*, pin the quilt top to the back with right sides together. Stitch around the sides and curved foot edge, making a ⅜" seam. Turn right side out and turn the border over to the front. The quilt can be finished with machine quilting, or with a scalloped edging or ruffle tucked under the border piece before it is stitched down.

fig 4

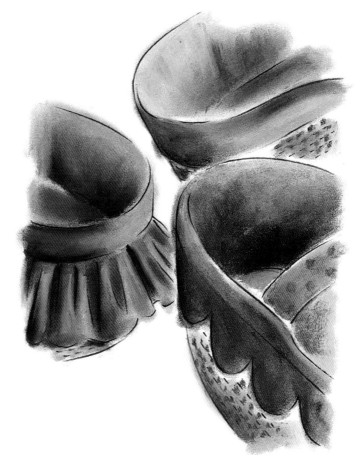

fig 5

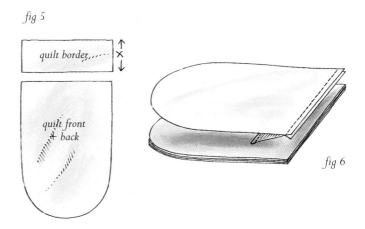

quilt border

quilt front & back

fig 6

A TRIO OF CUT-VELVET PILLOWS GAIN ADDED ELEGANCE FROM RICH TRIMMINGS—SILKEN TASSELS AND

CORDING AND GLASS BEADS.

See pages 158–60 for pillows.

renaissance

tapestry & tassels
for sumptuous dining rooms

In the courts of 16th-century Europe, clothing became extravagant. Aristocratic men spent huge sums on velvet suits trimmed with silver, on silk hats, and on jewelry. Cloaks were faced with gold or silver lace and even pearls. Ladies wore hooped or padded skirts and scented gloves. Even slippers were bejeweled.

At this time houses, formerly rather barren affairs, began to reflect the changing tastes. Rich tapestries hung on walls, beds became four-postered kingdoms, embroidered pillows and bolsters came into use, and Turkish rugs brightened great halls. Life was becoming more comfortable, attractive, and physically warmer than it had been in the past.

Introduce a glimpse of this splendid age into your house—without going overboard—with touches such as a pile of Elizabethan-style pillows or puddling draperies. Choose rich brocades and fringe them with tassels or braid. Dress velvet cushions with glossy cord or opt for lengths of lace or raw silk.

Raid boxes of remnants in fabric shops for brocade, velvet and taffeta (remnant boxes are always full of affordable treasures that can spark ideas). Use your finds all over the house for eye-catching details—pillows, curtain tiebacks, valances and even place mats. Update the traditionally somber 16th-century shades with more modern colors of bronze, beige, purple, black and dark red.

SCRAPS FROM OLD CURTAINS AND DRESSES CAN BE REMADE INTO ORNATE PILLOWS SUCH AS THIS FLAT-ENDED BOLSTER.

See page 163 for the flat-ended bolster.

fabric finery
for master baths

A master bathroom can and should be much more than a purely functional space. It should be a retreat, a place for luxurious scented baths taken by candlelight. Transform your master bath into a royal boudoir that will help you face the cold world outside.

The era that perfected the art of boudoir decoration was the 18th century, when women did not merely dress for a party, they armed themselves with the accessories of beauty to do battle in the ballroom. Follow their lead by treating a bathroom more as a room—complete with furnishings and fabric. A fabric screen is indispensable—offering moveable color, privacy and beauty. Tuck it in front of the bath to create a room within a room. Drape the walls in floor-length toiles or other antique print fabrics in glowing colors. Fabric-covered walls not only look sumptuous, they make the room physically warmer as well. Simply stitch your fabric into floor-to-ceiling panels and either staple or affix the panels with braids and pretty ribbons to molding or boards.

below

ELEGANT DETAILS ALSO HELP MAKE A BATHROOM A RETREAT. A TEXTURED THROW FIXED TO A CURTAIN RAIL WITH METAL CLIPS CREATES A SPLENDID ENTRANCE. FINE MUSLIN CURTAINS EDGED WITH RED BALL FRINGE ECHO THE COLORS IN THE TOILE TABLE SKIRT.

left

MORE THAN A PLACE TO WASH, THIS BATH IS A BOUDOIR TO LUXURIATE IN. THE COMBINATION OF FABRIC-COVERED WALLS AND A SCREEN TRANSFORM THIS MASTER BATHROOM.

See page 143 for fabric panels. For the stool seat, see page 55.

a living room
for wintry-day lounging

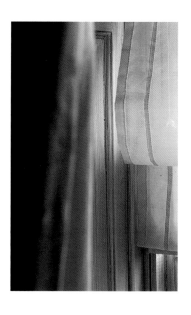

Fabrics can be an expensive proposition. But do not turn your back on a lavish look simply because the fabrics you love are too pricey. Instead, put your imagination to work. You can always do a Scarlett O'Hara and turn old curtains, for example, to new uses. Vintage dresses are another option. Scour antique stores, flea markets and thrift shops for materials suitable for a reincarnation. Alternatively, search out less-expensive printed fabrics, such as cotton toile and florals, or plain silk linings and Indian printed silks or even brilliantly hued synthetics for your projects.

This living room offers proof of the flexibility of unusual fabrics. Despite the scarcity of sunlight, the room glows even on the dreariest of days. Translucent, golden roman shades made of an organza-type material dress one set of windows. When the sun does shine, the shades create a sunny ambiance in the room. Moss-green raw silk curtains drape the other windows, teamed with a free-flowing layer of brilliant yellow silk under-curtains that share the same curtain pole. A woven damask that could have been made from an old curtain converts a dime-a-dozen director's chair into an object of beauty.

above

A TAILORED SHEER ROMAN SHADE CASTS A WARM GLOW OVER THE LIVING ROOM WHEN THE MORNING SUN COMES THROUGH. THE SHADE ALSO SCREENS AN UNSIGHTLY VIEW WITHOUT BLOCKING THE PRECIOUS LIGHT.

See pages 146–7 for the roman shade.

left

MIX AND MATCH FABRICS TO BRING DRAMA TO DRAPERIES. THESE CURTAINS ARE MADE UP OF TWO DIFFERENT WEIGHTS OF SILK IN CONTRASTING COLORS—CHEERY YELLOW AND MOSS GREEN.

See pages 148–52 for curtains.

right

THIS GOLDEN DAMASK SLIPCOVER DISGUISES AN ORDINARY DIRECTOR'S CHAIR. NOW IT HAS THE SOLEMN BEAUTY OF A MONK'S ROBE—COMPLETE WITH COWL. CURTAIN LININGS USUALLY REMAIN IN THE BACKGROUND—BUT NOT ON THESE WINDOWS. GOLDEN SILK LINING OFFERS A SHARP CONTRAST TO THE DEEP GREEN DRAPERIES.

See pages 176 for director's chair with hood and 148–52 for curtains.

my lady's chamber
the making of a bedroom

During the Renaissance, the creation of the four-poster bed was an important—and also romantic—innovation in terms of comfort in drafty castles. Curtains were draped from the top rails; the tester roof was often an ornate tapestry. Headboards were huge and extravagantly carved, sometimes with little nooks for candles; mattresses were stuffed with wool or feathers as opposed to straw.

Today, the coverings on the bed still set the tone of the room. This bedroom, for example, has all the drama and excitement of a Far Eastern bazaar thanks to a rich array of embroidered fabrics and a velvet-and-silk throw on the 19th-century walnut bed. Scattered Oriental rugs contribute to the mood as do crinkled red silk curtains edged in striped silks in exotic colors. A mirror between the two windows multiplies the amount of light and creates the illusion of space. The white ceiling offers a visual break from the vivid yellow walls.

above left

A COCKTAIL DRESS OF A SLIPCOVER (SEWN IN DROP-DEAD RED TAFFETA) SHOWS OFF THE SHAPELY LINES OF A SLIPPER CHAIR.

See pages 176–7 for bedroom chair and 162 for piped bolster with gathered ends.

left

A COMFORTABLE READING CHAIR CLAIMS A SPOT BY THE FIREPLACE. ITS SLIPCOVER IS SEWN IN A STURDY WOVEN FABRIC THAT UNITES ALL THE ROOM'S VIBRANT COLORS.

See pages 178–80 for slipcover for armchair.

A WIDE RUFFLED BORDER OF TANGY YELLOW, VIVID ORANGE, AND A TOUCH OF LIME MAKES A

SHOWSTOPPER OUT OF BURGUNDY SILK CURTAINS. TASSELED TIEBACKS ADD ANOTHER ELABORATE TOUCH

TO THE BALLROOM DRAPES. THE MOSES BASKET IS EQUALLY LUXURIOUS WHEN LINED IN TAFFETA WITH A

SCALLOPED VELVET COVERLET.

See pages 136–7 for baby baskets.

techniques & projects

Anyone who is familiar with basic sewing and dressmaking should have no problems undertaking any of the projects in this book. This section introduces the special techniques that will give a professional finish to your work, and includes clear and detailed explanations of how to make the various home furnishings featured, from a simple napkin or pillowcase to a slipcover for an armchair.

basic techniques

seams

An accurate seam requires careful preparation. Pin together both layers of fabric at 2-4″ intervals, with pins at right angles to edge. Baste together with a contrasting thread, just inside seamline. If the fabric is liable to ravel, finish raw edges with a zigzag stitch before seaming, taking care not to stretch fabric edges.

plain seam

Pin and baste the two pieces with right sides together and raw edges even, then stitch along the seamline. Secure each end of the seam with a few reverse stitches. Remove basting thread and press seam allowances open from the back *(fig 1)*.

corners

To sew around a right-angled corner, lift the presser foot, leaving the needle down. Turn the fabric 90 degrees, lower the foot, and continue. Clip the seam allowance before turning right side out. On sharp corners, work one or two stitches across the point. Cut across the allowance, then trim back each side. For inside corners, snip into the allowance, to within ⅟₁₆″ of the stitching *(fig 2)*.

curved seams

To reduce bulk, trim the seam allowance to ¼″. For an outside curve, cut a series of regularly spaced notches to within ⅟₁₆″ of the stitching so that the seam will lie flat when pressed open. On an inside curve, clip the allowance *(fig 3)*.

french seam

The second line of stitching on this double seam encloses the raw edges, which makes it hard-wearing and suitable for fabrics where a seam allowance would show through. With wrong sides together, pin and stitch ¼″ from the edge. Trim to ⅛″, then refold with right sides together. Sew again, ⅜″ from the edge *(fig 4)*.

flat fell seam

This strong double seam is reversible and will stand up to hard wear and washing. With wrong sides together, stitch ⅝″ from the edge. Press the allowance to one side. Trim the lower edge to ¼″. Press under ⅛″ along the upper edge. Fold the upper edge over the lower edge and stitch down close to the fold *(fig 5)*.

slip stitch

This makes a neat seam between two folded edges. The needle passes through the folds so that only a small amount of thread shows. Butt the edges together and bring the needle through one fold and into the opposite side. Make a ¼″ stitch within the fold, bring the needle out and back into the other edge *(fig 6)*.

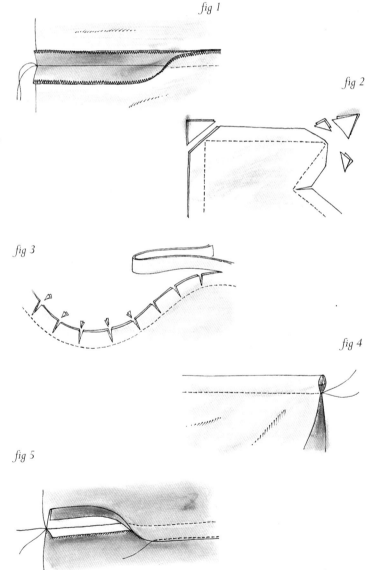

fig 1

fig 2

fig 3

fig 4

fig 5

fig 6

hems

The way in which an edge is finished depends on the weight of the fabric. A thick material should only have a single hem with one turn. A double hem with one narrow and one deep turn is suited to most materials, while a hem which has two equal turns is used to give a firmer edge or for sheer fabrics *(fig 1)*. Most hems can be machine-stitched, but curtains generally are stitched by hand.

single hem

Zigzag the raw edge, or trim with pinking shears. Turn up to the right length, pin and stitch. To sew by hand, use herringbone stitch: starting at the left-hand side, take the needle diagonally upward. Make a short horizontal stitch into the main fabric, from right to left. Take the needle down to the right and make the next horizontal stitch through the hem *(fig 2)*. Continue to the end.

double hem

Turn up to the right length. Press under ¼" along the raw edge and pin. For equal turns, turn up measurement twice. Sew by hand with hemming stitch: work from right to left, picking up two or three threads from the wrong side for each small stitch *(fig 3)*. Do not pull the thread too tightly. For a neater hem, after picking up threads, slide the needle back into the hem fold as for a slip stitch and bring it out to the left for the next stitch.

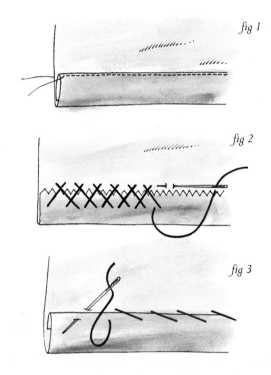

fig 1

fig 2

fig 3

mitering

When two hems meet at a corner, the surplus fabric can be finished with a miter. For a single hem, press under the allowance along each side and unfold. Fold over the corner at a 45-degree angle, so that the creases line up to form a square *(fig 4)*, then refold hems to form miter. Slipstitch the folded edges. For a double hem, press under both allowances. Undo the second fold and turn in as above. Refold into a miter *(fig 5)*.

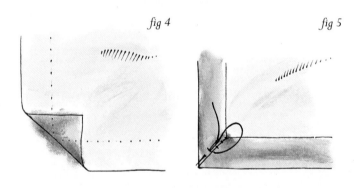

fig 4   *fig 5*

binding

Binding is used to finish the edges of thick or quilted fabrics. Straight sides can be bound with fabric cut along the grain, but the flexibility of bias binding is needed on a curve. Ready-made bindings are available, but it is easy to make your own. Cut the strips twice the finished width plus ½" for the seam allowances.

cutting bias strips

Draw a diagonal line across the fabric at 45 degrees to the edge. Mark a series of lines parallel to the diagonal, the required width apart, and cut along these lines. Join the strips together at right angles, ¼" from the edge *(fig 6)*. Press open and trim the corners.

To make a long strip, cut a 12" x 24" rectangle. Cut off one corner at 45 degrees and sew it to the opposite straight edge. Rule a series of lines parallel to the diagonal edge *(fig 7)*. With right sides facing, match "a" to "b," pin and stitch. Turn right side out and cut along the now-continuous line *(fig 8)*.

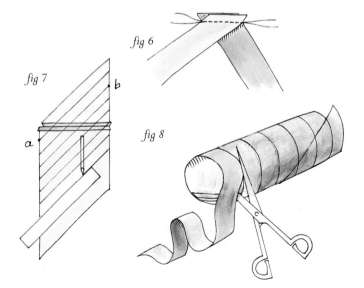

fig 6

fig 7

fig 8

attaching binding

Press under ¼″ along each long edge, then press in half lengthwise with wrong sides together. Fold over the edge of the fabric and pin, mitering corners and easing curves. Machine-stitch close to the outer fold, making sure that the stitching goes through all the layers, or slipstitch in place *(fig 9)*. On quilts, unfold binding and, right sides together and matching ¼″ foldline to quilt seamline, pin and stitch binding to quilt front. Fold binding to quilt back, fold under ¼″ and slipstitch along machine stitching line.

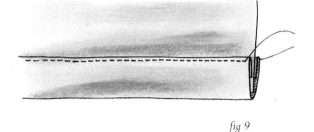

fig 9

piping

Piping cord, covered with a bias fabric strip, is sewn into a seam as reinforcement and decoration. On slipcovers it is used to outline the shape of a chair, and an edge of contrasting piping adds visual interest to a pillow cover. The cord can be bought in several thicknesses and should be boiled before use if it is not preshrunk.

covering the cord

Cut a bias strip to the required length: the total length of the seams, plus an extra 2″ for each joining seam. The width of the strip should equal the circumference of the cord, plus 1¼″. With the right side facing out, fold the strip around the cord and pin. Stitch in place, using a zipper or cording foot *(fig 10)*.

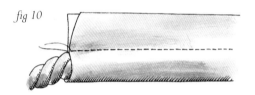

fig 10

piping a seam

Pin the piping to the right side of the fabric, matching the raw edges. Baste, then stitch with a zipper foot. Clip into the seam allowance at any corners, and stitch around it in a curve, not at an angle. Notch the allowance on both piping and main fabric around a curved edge *(fig 11)*. Right sides together and matching edges, pin the second piece of fabric to the first, enclosing piping. Stitch just inside the previous stitch line.

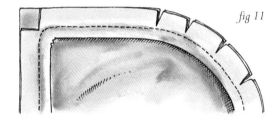

fig 11

making a round of piping

A continuous length of piping, such as that on a pillow cover, has to have an inconspicuous final seam. It should be positioned next to a seamline if possible. Sew the piping in place, leaving 2″ unstitched on each side of the seam. Remove the stitching that encloses the cord for 1¼″ at each end. Trim the cord so that the ends butt together and bind with sewing thread. Trim the bias strip so that one end overlaps the other by ⅝″. Turn under ¼″ at this end and fold over the raw end *(fig 12)*. Slipstitch the seam and sew the piping to the seamline.

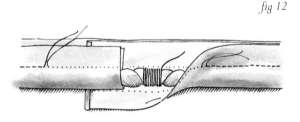

fig 12

decorative cords

Decorative silky cords are sewn by hand along a finished seam. Use matching thread and stitch through a few strands at the back of the cord. Cord cannot be joined neatly, so when it is applied to a pillow cover, the two ends are concealed within the seam. Allow an extra 2″ of cord and leave a 1¼″ opening in the seam stitching. Partially unravel one end of the cord and insert into the opening *(fig 13)*. Stitch the rest around the edge and unravel the remaining end so that it lies flat. Tuck it into the opening next to the first end, then stitch securely in place.

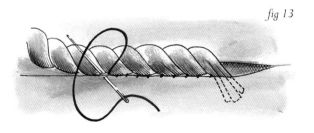

fig 13

braids & fringes

Woven braids and fringes may be attached by hand or machine. If the trimming does not fray, the ends can be joined with a narrow seam; otherwise they should be overlapped and hidden inside the seam *(fig 1)*. Allow an extra 2″ at each end for this. When a fringe is used to border a throw, make it reversible by turning up a single hem on the right side and stitching the trimming to conceal the raw edge.

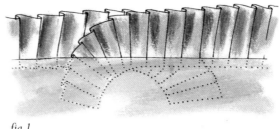

fig 1

gathers & pleats

Gathered and pleated ruffles have many applications; they can soften the edge of a window shade, add a formal border to a slipcover, or a flouncy skirt to a tablecloth. They may be double for extra fullness – simply cut the strip to twice the required width and fold in half – or single, with a narrow hem along the lower edge. Join the fabric with a plain seam for a double ruffle or a flat fell seam for a single ruffle.

gathering

Fabric is drawn up with a thread sewn along one edge. With a lightweight fabric, run two parallel rows of long straight machine stitch, or use a double length of thread to sew a running stitch. On a heavy fabric or for a long length, use zigzag gathering to prevent the thread from breaking. Set the machine to a long narrow satin stitch and sew just inside the seam allowance. Secure a length of buttonhole thread around a pin at the start. Hold the thread under the presser foot as you sew, so that it is couched down by the zigzag *(fig 2)*, then pull it up to gather.

attaching gathers

It is important that the gathering be distributed equally. When a ruffle is to go onto a single edge, fold it in half, then quarters. Mark these divisions with notches at the top. Do the same with the edge of the main fabric. Sew a separate gathering thread for each quarter of the ruffle. With right sides together, pin the ruffle to the main fabric, so that the notches match. Pull up each thread to the proper length, adjust the gathers so that they are even, and pin *(fig 3)*. Knot the gathering threads before sewing. Finish the raw edges with a zigzag.

This method is also used for a continuous ruffle. For a square, the frill is folded into four, and one quarter sewn to each side. For a rectangle – a pillowcase or tablecloth – add up the length of the four sides and divide the number by eight. Make notches this distance apart around the perimeter, starting at one corner. Fold the ruffle into eighths, and notch the top edge. Gather between each pair of notches, and pin *(fig 4)*. Allow extra fullness at each corner. A ruffle is attached to a bedspread by measuring the sides and bottom edge in the same way.

self-bound ruffle

Conceal the raw edges of the ruffle to give a neat finish to a bed drape or curtain. Trim the gathered edge to ¼″ and press under ¼″ along the seam allowance of the main fabric. Fold the allowance over the gathers and slipstitch or machine-stitch in place *(fig 5)*.

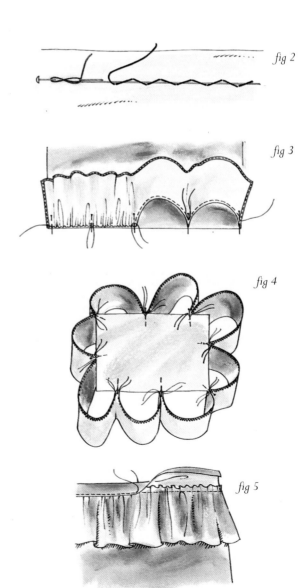

fig 2

fig 3

fig 4

fig 5

pleating

A strip of fabric for a pleated edge must be cut across the width of the fabric, following the grain, so that it will hang straight. Make sure any seams lie at the back of a fold and that the pleats line up with the corners on chairs or dust ruffles.

knife pleats

Cut a strip of fabric twice the finished length. With tailor's chalk, mark a series of lines the same width apart as one pleat. Match points "a" to points "c" so all the pleats lie in the same direction *(fig 6)*. Pin, then baste in place along the top edge.

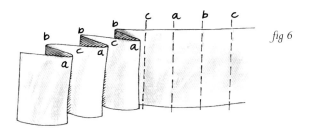

fig 6

box pleats

Two knife pleats folded toward each other form a box pleat — allow three times the finished length. Chalk parallel lines at right angles to the edge so that the distance between them is half the finished width of the pleat. Matching "a" to "c," then "e" to "c," pin each pleat *(fig 7)*, then baste along the top edge.

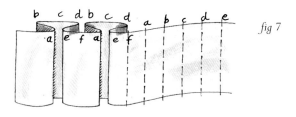

fig 7

fabric panels

There are several quick methods of using lengths of fabric which involve little sewing and which give instant results. A hemmed rectangle can be draped over a curtain pole as a swag, or pinned at ceiling height to cover a wall.

matching patterned fabrics

When patterned fabrics are joined, the design has to match up horizontally across the seam. Make sure the pattern starts at the same point on each piece. Press under the seam allowance along one side. Pin to the second length so that the motifs match. Stitch together: bring the needle through one fold and into the other side. Make a ½″ stitch, parallel to the folded edge. Take the needle back into the fold. Make a ½″ stitch inside, and continue down the seam *(fig 8)*. Place right sides together and machine-stitch along the basted line.

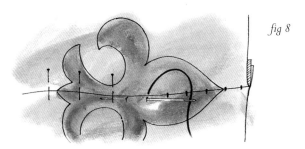

fig 8

joining fabric lengths

To avoid an intrusive center seam, cut the second piece of fabric lengthwise into two panels and sew one to each side of the main piece *(fig 9)*.

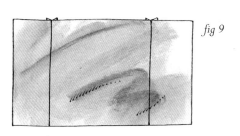

fig 9

bagging

To make reversible panels, pin two pieces with right sides together. For a throw, sew around all four sides, leaving a 10″ opening at one edge. Clip the corners, turn right side out, and slipstitch the opening. For curtains, sew the side and bottom edges, clip the corners, and turn. Finish the top edge with header tape or loops.

fabric-covered panels

Fabric can simply be stretched over a screen or padded headboard. Cut fabric 2″ larger all around than the area to be covered. Staple the fabric to the center of each side, leaving a margin of 2″ and keeping it taut. Working out, secure at 4″ intervals, checking that the grain is not distorted *(fig 10)*. Trim surplus fabric and glue braid around the edge to conceal the raw edges.

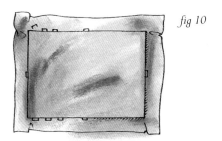

fig 10

fastenings

Fastenings can be hidden away, like a practical zipper at the back of a pillow cover, or, like ties or bows, made into a decoration in their own right.

zippers

Metal and nylon zippers are available in various lengths, weights, and colors for all purposes. The length is always measured along the teeth. Use a zipper foot to sew in place, stitching ⅛" from the teeth.

inserting a zipper in a plain seam

Baste the two sides together along the seam allowance. Machine stitch at each end, leaving a central opening ½" longer than the zipper. Work a few reverse stitches to reinforce the ends of the stitching. Press open and place the zipper, face down, along the basted seam. Pin and baste, then stitch in place from the right side *(fig 1)*.

inserting a zipper in a piped seam

Seam the two sides to the point where the zipper is to be inserted. Open the zipper and, with right sides together, baste and sew one side along the piped edge, so the teeth lie next to the cord *(fig 2)*. Turn the seam allowance to the wrong side and close the zipper. Press under the allowance on the other side of the seam and line the folded edge up with the piping. Baste the second side of the zipper to the inside of the fold, and sew in place ¼" from edge and across the end *(fig 3)*.

ties

For each tie, cut a strip of fabric, measuring the finished length and twice the finished width, plus ⅜" added all around.

For narrow ties press under ⅜" along each edge including the ends, then press in half lengthwise. Baste, then machine-stitch all around, ⅛" from the edge *(fig 4)*.

For wide ties fold in half lengthwise with right sides together, and stitch the long edge. Press so the seam lies down the center, then sew across one end, straight or diagonally *(fig 5)*. Trim excess fabric and clip corners. Turn right side out and press.

bows

An ornamental bow is made from four separate pieces. Detailed measurements are given with projects, but follow this method to make a bow of any size *(fig 6)*.

Main part: width = 2b, length = 2a, plus ⅝" all around

Tails: cut two, width = 2d, length = c, plus ⅝" all around

Center: width = e, length = b, plus ⅝" all around

Fold the main part in half lengthwise with right sides together and seam the long edges. Turn right side out and press with the seam at center back. Repeat for the center piece. Turn the ends of the main part to the middle and sew two gathering threads through all the layers *(fig 7)*. Pull up and secure. Make the tails as for a wide tie above. Press and sew to the back of the main part, on each side of the gathers *(fig 8)*. Stitch the center around gathers and over tails, securing at the back.

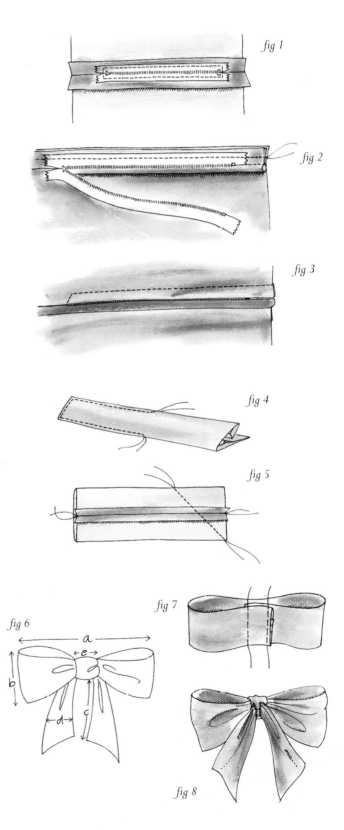

fig 1

fig 2

fig 3

fig 4

fig 5

fig 6

fig 7

fig 8

shades

The way you cover your windows will set the tone for the whole room. Curtains, draperies, shades and valances can be used in combination, not just for privacy and insulation from sound and darkness, but to add drama, life, and light. Creating your own may seem to be a daunting task, but it can be as simple as sewing lengths of tape to the top of a hemmed panel.

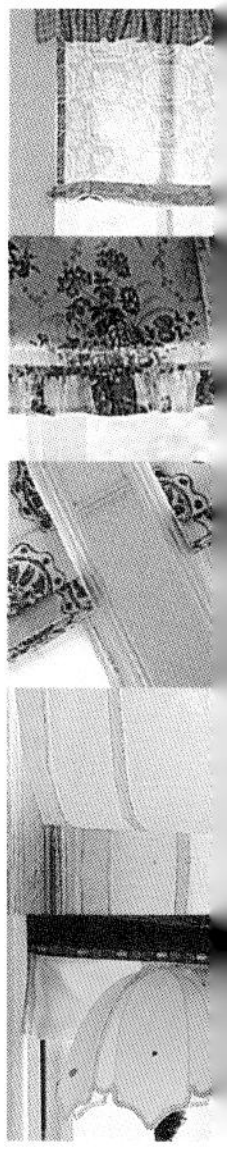

Shades can be used on their own for an uncluttered look, or hung behind coordinating curtains. Unlined swedish-style shades roll up from the lower edge where a dowel supports the hem, and work well with patterned or semi-sheer fabrics since there are no rods to show through. Roman shades are pulled up into pleats by a system of cords which run through rows of small rings secured to the reverse side. Those stitched directly to the fabric give a soft, unstructured look; on wooden rods the cloth falls into more formal pleats. When choosing fabric, bear in mind that a roman shade will be raised for much of the day; large repeats may not work well when they are folded.

Swedish and roman shades suit both large and small windows, but should not be wider than 6', or the rods will bend under the weight of the fabric. Ideally, a shade should be cut from a single width of material. If fabrics have to be joined, sew half of the extra width to each side of center panel to avoid a seam in the middle. Using a contrasting color for the two edges makes the additional fabric into a decorative feature. An ornamental finish such as a ruffle or a scalloped edging can be added to the bottom (see p.142), but position the first row of rings slightly higher than usual, so that the edge will show below the folds when the shade is pulled up.

measuring (fig 1)

Both types of shades are attached with Velcro to a fabric-covered wooden strip which can be screwed directly inside the window recess, or mounted on the wall above the window using angle brackets. Decide where you want your shade to hang before determining the finished width and length (a & b). The lining and main fabrics must be cut accurately along the grain, so that the shade will hang straight.

For a shade that fits within the window, a = the width of the recess (c) and b = the length from the top of the recess to the sill (d).

For a shade that fits beyond the window recess, a = the width of the window frame plus the desired distance at each side (e), and b = the length from the top of the wooden strip including the desired height of shade above window to the desired length below the sill (f).

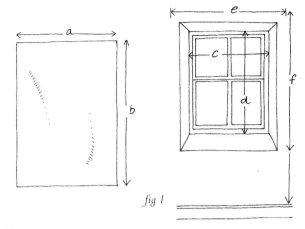

fig 1

swedish shade

materials

Main fabric, ½"-diameter dowel (length = a -½"), 1"-wide Velcro (length = a -½"), fine cotton piping cord, (length = 6b + a), two glass or metal rings 1¼" in diameter, 15¾" x ¾" strip of leather or woven tape

For mounting: wooden strips 1" x 2" (length = a - ½") extra fabric to cover strips, staple gun, 2 x ½" screw eyes, tacks, hammer, cleat

measuring & cutting out (fig 1)

Main fabric: width = a + 2½", length = b + 2"

making

1 Press under and stitch a 1¼" double hem along each side of the shade. Make a 1¼" double hem along the lower edge. Insert the dowel through this channel and slipstitch the ends to hold it in place *(fig 2)*.

2 At the top edge, press ¾" to the wrong side. Pin the hooked side of the Velcro strip so that it conceals the raw edge and stitch it in place *(fig 3)*.

mounting & cording

3 Cover the wooden strip with fabric to match the shade, folding at the ends like a gift-wrapped package. Staple the other side of the Velcro to one narrow side and screw an eye underneath a point 2" in from each edge *(fig 4)*. Mount the strip so that the Velcro faces the room.

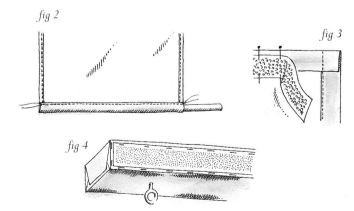

fig 2

fig 3

fig 4

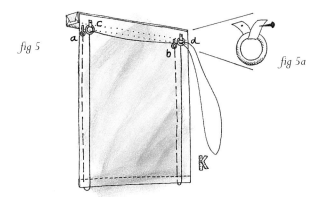

fig 5

fig 5a

4 Attach the shade to the strip along the Velcro strips. Cut the tape or leather strip in half and thread each piece through one of the rings *(fig 5a)*. Attach one to each side of the shade heading, 2″ in from the edge *(fig 5)*.

5 To thread the pull cord, tie one end of the piping cord to the screw eye at "a," then bring the other end under the shade and back up through ring "c" at the front. Tie the other end securely to the second screw eye at "b," then thread the double cord forward through ring "d" at the front to form the pull *(fig 5)*. Screw the cleat to the wall at the right-hand side at windowsill level.

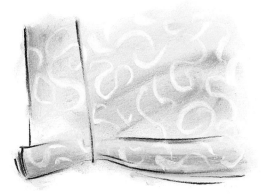

roman shades

Decide how many folds your shade is to have; depending on the proportions of the window, there are usually four or five. Deduct 2″ (z) from the finished length, to allow space for it to be pulled up, and calculate the length between the rods or rings.

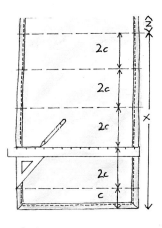

● determining the distance between the folds

For a shade without rods: divide length "x" by twice the number of folds plus one, to find length "c." The first row of loops will be this distance from the lower edge and subsequent rows will be 2c apart *(fig 6)*.

For a shade with rods: subtract 2″ for each rod from length "x," then divide by twice the number of folds plus one for length "c." The first fold will be this distance from the lower edge and the following folds will be at 2c + 2″ intervals.

fig 6

soft roman shade

This is the most basic roman shade, which falls into loose folds. An unlined shade allows in some daylight, so select a lightweight fabric with a firm weave.

materials

Main fabric, approx 15 x 1″ rings, ½″-diameter dowel (length = a -½″), yardstick and carpenter's square, fade-away pen or chalk pencil

measuring & cutting out (see fig 1)

Main fabric: width = a + 1½″, length = b + 3¼″

fig 7

making

1 Press under and stitch a ¾″ double hem along the two sides of the shade. Make a 1¼″ double hem (equal turns) along the lower edge, mitering the corners (see p. 140). At lower edge insert the rod under the miters, and slipstitch in place (see *fig 2*).

2 Figure out the distance between the rows of rings (see below left), then mark the fold lines on the back of the shade using a carpenter's square and yardstick *(fig 6)*. Make each measurement from the bottom edge to ensure the lines are parallel.

3 Using matching thread, sew the rings on in rows of three along marked lines, one 2″ in from each side edge and one in the center *(fig 7)*. Finish the top edge of the shade with Velcro as for step 2 of the Swedish Shade.

formal roman shade

The more formal pleats of this shade are supported by a series of rods inserted into narrow channels made by folding and stitching the fabric. Stitch each line in the same direction so that the fabric does not pull.

materials

As for the Soft Roman Shade, plus ½″-diameter dowel (length = a -½″) for each channel, ¾″ wooden lath (length = a -½″) instead of dowel for bottom channel

measuring & cutting out (see fig 1)

Width = a + 3″

Length = b + 3¼″, + 2″ for each rod channel

making

1 Press under and stitch a ¾" double hem (equal turns) along the two sides of
the shade. Make a 1¼" double hem (equal turns) along the bottom edge. Miter,
but do not stitch down the corners. Press, then place the shade face down on the
work surface. Work out the distance between the rods and mark on the reverse
side as for step 2 of the Soft Roman Shade.

2 Fold along the first line and press lightly. Pin the two sides together at right
angles to the fold and stitch 1" from it *(fig 8)*. Repeat for the other channels.

3 Insert one rod into each channel and slipstitch the open ends to keep them
in place. Slip the lath into the bottom channel under the mitered corners, and
slipstitch them together. Sew three rings to each channel, one 4" in from each
side and the third in the center. Stitch them securely to the folded edge *(fig 9)*.
Finish the top edge of the shade with Velcro as for step 2 of the Swedish Shade.

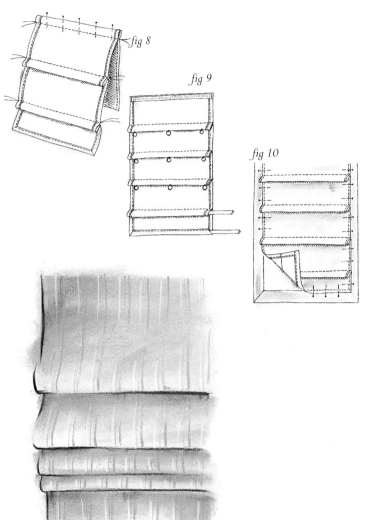

fig 8

fig 9

fig 10

lined roman shade

The additional layer of fabric gives this shade a tailored appearance. The rods are
attached to the lining, which is made in the same way as the formal shade. It is
hand sewn to the main fabric, so that no stitch lines are visible from the front.

materials

As for the Soft Roman Shade, plus lining fabric

measuring & cutting out (see fig 1)

Main fabric: width = a + 4¾", length = b + 3⅛"

Lining: width = a, length = b + 2" for each channel

making

1 Press under, then pin and baste a single hem of 1¼" along each side edge of
the lining fabric. Mark and sew the stitching lines on right side, as for steps 1 and
2 of the Formal Roman Shade. Pin and baste a single hem of 1¼" at lower edge.

2 Press under a single hem of 2⅜" along each side and the lower edge of the
main fabric, mitering the corners. Sew in place with herringbone stitch.

3 Lay the main fabric face down on the work surface. Place the lining on top,
with the channels facing up. Line up the corners and seams so that it is
positioned ¾" from top and 1¼" from other edges; pin in place *(fig 10)*. Leaving an
opening to insert lath at bottom, slipstitch the lining to the shade.

4 Insert the rods and lath and finish as for step 3 of the Formal Roman Shade.

● cording & mounting roman shades

The same technique is used for all three roman shade variations.

materials

Thin polyester cord (length = 6b + 2a), length of 1" x 2" wooden strip (½"
shorter than finished width), 3 screw eyes, 2 angle brackets or 2 large screws,
staple gun or hammer and tacks, cleat, wooden weighted cord pull

method

Cover the strip and attach the Velcro
as for the Swedish Shade (see
fig 3 on page 145). Mount above the
window or into the recess, using a
carpenter's level to keep it straight.
Screw the eyes to the underside so
that they line up with the rows of
loops. Velcro the shade to the batten.

fig 11

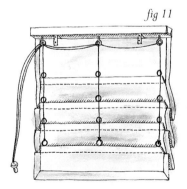

threading the cords (fig 11)

Cut the cord into equal lengths. Standing between the window and the back of
the shade, knot left cord securely to the first loop on the bottom rod, then
thread it up the row and through the screw eye. Thread the middle cord in the
same way and pass the end to the left and through the first screw eye. Do the
same with the last cord, so that all the ends pass through the left screw eye. Knot
the cords together at sill level and trim the ends even. Attach the cord pull.

curtains

When deciding which fabric and type of heading to use for curtains, bear in mind the proportions of the window and the size of the room. Brocade drapes with a pencil-pleat heading, topped by a matching shaped valance, may be ideal for a large, high-ceilinged living room, while short, café curtains will look pretty in a country dining room. Bedroom curtains should be lined to keep out the light in the early morning. Curtains are not just for windows; they can also be made to hang on a bedframe, or across a door opening or screen.

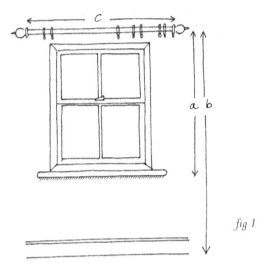

fig 1

tracks & poles

The type of hardware – track, rod, or pole – will influence the look of the finished curtain. Make sure it is at least 8″ longer than the width of the window so the curtains can clear the frame when they are pulled back.

Decorative poles, which are supported on brackets above the window, come in many styles: wrought iron with curled ends, wood with turned finials, or shiny brass. Curtains can be hung directly on the pole with ties or loops, or using hooks attached to large rings that are threaded onto the pole.

Curtain tracks can be mounted on the wall or ceiling above the window and are attached at several points along their length to give adequate support. They usually lie near the wall, but deeper fixtures are available to allow space for a shade to be set behind the curtains. An overlap arm in the center means the curtains can be pulled together neatly, and a track with a pull-cord system for heavyweight curtains will mean they do not need to be pulled by hand.

measuring *(fig 1)*

Hardware should be in place before you measure. Decide how long you want the curtains to be: above or below the windowsill, skimming or touching the floor, or somewhere in between. Then choose the heading. This will affect the fullness – a gathered, sheer fabric will require more widths than a lined panel, and a large-scale pattern may look more effective if it hangs flat.

calculating fabric amounts

This may seem complicated, but the rules are straightforward. Reputable fabric suppliers usually have staff who can help you work out how much you need.

length

The basic length is the distance between the fixture and the bottom of the curtain (a or b). To this are added the allowances for the heading and hem. If you are using patterned fabric, allow extra so the design lines up across the seams and both curtains in a pair will match. Measure the height of the repeat and add this measurement to each length.

width

A curtain for a tall window will need to be fuller than one for a small window so the fabric can hang in proper folds. Multiply the length of the track (c) by the fullness needed for the chosen heading (see p.150). Divide this figure by the fabric width: most fabrics are a standard 44″ wide, but check first. This gives the number of fabric lengths needed for the window (round partial numbers upward to next whole number).

Multiply the curtain length by the number of lengths needed to find the total amount. The measurement for lining is the same as for the main fabric, but need not include any allowance made for pattern repeats or headers.

cutting out & joining

All cut edges must be straight so that the curtains will hang properly. Lay the fabric flat on a clean surface, measure the length accurately, and use sharp, long-bladed shears to cut out. For solid fabrics cut carefully across the weave – it may help to pull out a single thread to achieve a straight line. Follow the pattern lines on printed fabrics, marking a chalk guideline with a ruler and carpenter's square if necessary. When you are making a pair of curtains, any half widths to be added should be sewn to the outside edge of the main pieces.

Always cut off the selvages before joining fabric widths to remove any lettering and to prevent pulling. For lined curtains, use a flat open seam or, if they are to remain unlined, a double seam which conceals the raw edges. Pin solid fabrics together with right sides facing and stitch along the seamline. Stripes and checks have to be matched up first. Patterned fabrics are more complicated; they must line up horizontally across the seam (see p.143). When cutting the lengths, make sure the pattern starts at the same point at the top of each drop.

unlined curtains

An unlined curtain is simply a rectangular piece of fabric which has been hemmed and mitered around three sides, then finished along the top edge with a heading.

measuring & cutting out (see fig 1)

Calculate the amount of fabric (see left). Add 5″ to the finished width for side hems, and 6″ to the length for the hem, plus the heading allowance.

making

1   With right sides together, join the widths of fabric with a french or flat fell seam (see p.139). Press under a 1¼″ double hem (equal turns) along each side and a 3″ double hem on the lower edge.

mitering the corner

2   Mark three points with pins; one at the corner, one on the inside edge of the side hem where it meets the bottom, and the corresponding point on the hem *(fig 2)*. Unfold all the creases, then refold so there is a single turn along both edges. Fold the corner in so all three points line up *(fig 3)* and refold the side and hem to form a miter. Insert a curtain weight if required, then slipstitch the two sides together *(fig 4)* from the corner to the inner edge.

3   Sew or machine-stitch the side and hem allowances. Press the heading allowance to the wrong side and finish with your chosen heading.

fig 2

fig 3

fig 4

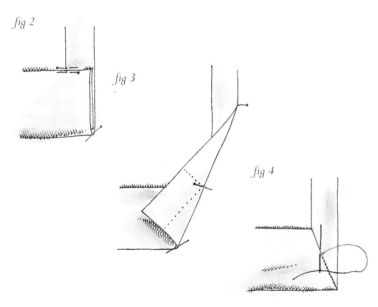

lined curtains

A lining is needed when you are making curtains from thicker fabric. In addition to improving the way the material drapes, it will provide insulation and prevent fading. If a curtain is to be seen from both the front and back – a bed hanging, for example – sew the two sides together using the bagging technique to make it reversible (see p.143).

loose-lined curtains

These curtains have a separate layer of fabric joined to the main fabric along the sides and the top edge, while the two hems remain separate.

measuring & cutting out (see fig 1)

Add an extra 2¾″ to the finished width of the main fabric. Add a 5″ hem, and a heading allowance to the length. Cut the lining so that it is 5″ shorter and 3″ narrower than the main fabric.

making

1   Join widths as required with a ⅝″ flat seam and press open. Fold both lining and main fabric in half along the top edge and mark the center points.

2   Matching the top edges, with right sides together, stitch the lining to the main fabric along each side edge, making a ⅝″ seam. Stitch to a point 6″ above the bottom edge of the lining. Press the seam allowance toward the lining center. Turn right side out and line up the two center points at the top. The side seams should now lie ¾″ in from the outer edges.

fig 5   *fig 6*

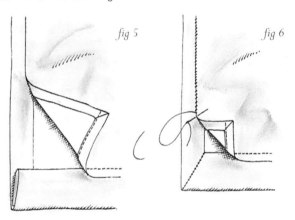

3   Press under a 1¼″ double hem on the lining *(fig 5)*. Mark the corners and the points where the side and hem meet and miter as in step 2 of the Unlined Curtain. Join the corners with slip stitch, then machine-stitch the hem.

4   Press under a 2½″ double hem (equal turns) along the lower edge of the main curtain *(fig 5)*, then miter the corners as before. Inserting a weight inside each improves the way the curtain hangs. Slipstitch the hem, then slipstitch the loose edges of the lining to the sides of the main curtain *(fig 6)*. Press the heading allowance to the wrong side and finish with your chosen heading.

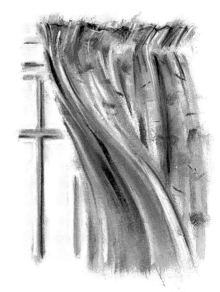

decorative headings

Curtain hooks and tracks are the traditional way of hanging curtains, but there are many quicker and less formal ways of attaching lined or unlined curtains to poles and rings using matching or contrasting ties, loops, and tapes.

cased heading

This heading slides over a curtain wire or café rod and is suitable for sheer fabrics, such as voile or organdy, and lightweight cottons.

measuring & cutting out

Allow up to three times the width of the finished curtain, depending on the weight of the fabric, and add 5″ to the finished length (more for a thick pole).

making the heading

Press under and pin a double 2½″ hem along the top edge. Machine-stitch a line 1¼″ from the top, then a second line 1″ further down to form the casing (*fig 7*). Slide the curtain onto the rod and position it. Use this method to cover a screen by making a second casing along the hem, with or without a ruffle.

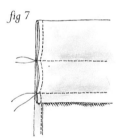
fig 7
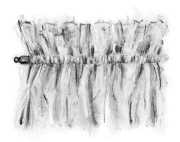

tape ties on straight heading

Ties can be tied to curtain rings or directly to a pole. The heading hem will drop forward when it is hung.

measuring & cutting out

Use 15″ lengths of ½″-wide cotton tape to make the ties. Divide the width of the curtain by the number of ties to make sure they are evenly spaced. They should be 5″-6″ apart. Add a heading allowance of 2½″ to the finished length.

making the heading

Press under a 1¼″ double hem (equal turns) along the top edge. Fold the first tie in half and slip the folded edge under the hem, ¾″ in from the outside edge. Pin the hem in place and add the other ties at regular intervals. Top-stitch the hem, securing the ties as you sew (*fig 8*).

fig 8

fabric ties on pleated heading

This softly pleated heading works best on sheer fabrics.

measuring & cutting out

The pleats are 5″-6″ (distance "a" on *fig 9*) apart. Calculate how many pleats will fit along the finished width, and add 4″ for each. Add a 6″ heading allowance to the finished length.

making the heading

Press under and stitch a 3″ double hem (equal turns) along the top edge. With a pin, mark a point which lies ½a from the top left corner. Mark a second point 4″ (z) away. Bring the two points together and pin at the top edge to make a pleat. Repeat at regular intervals along the top edge, placing the first pin distance "a" beyond the last fold (*fig 9*). Catch each pleat into position with a few secure stitches. Make a ¾″ x 10″ narrow fabric tie (see p.144) for each pleat. Fold in half and stitch in place.

fig 9 ⟨½a⟩⟨ a ⟩⟨ z ⟩
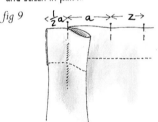

buttoned loops

These can be used to fasten curtains to a pole or to a stationary structure such as a bedframe.

measuring & cutting out

Calculate the spacing as for the tape ties at left. Depending on the thickness of the fabric and the size of the pole or frame, the finished loops should be about 1¼″ wide and 5″ long. Add a 1½″ heading allowance to the finished length. For each loop, cut a strip of fabric twice the finished length plus 2″ by twice the finished width plus 1¼″.

making the loops

fig 10

With wrong sides together, stitch the long edges together, making a ⅝″ seam. Press the seam open so it lies along the center and stitch along the top of the tube, ⅜″ in from the edge (*fig 10*). Clip the corners, turn right side out, and press. Make a buttonhole parallel to the closed edge on each loop.

making the heading

Press a ¾″ double hem (equal turns) to the wrong side along the top edge. With the seamed side of the loops facing up, slip unsewn end of the first loop under the fold and

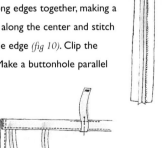
fig 11

pin. Pin the other loops at regular intervals, then stitch the hem down. Turn the loops up and pin *(fig 11)*, then topstitch along the upper edge to hold them upright. Sew a button to the base of each loop on the right side.

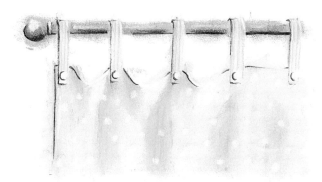

heading tapes

Heading tape is used both to gather a curtain and as a support for the hooks which attach the drapes to the track or to the rings on a pole. It comes in various weights and has continuous thick threads woven through it which can be pulled up to give the curtain its fullness, or left flat. Standard 1¼" tape is used for finer fabrics and you should allow 1½ to 2 times the width of the finished curtain. Pencil tape, 3" wide, gathers up into narrow pleats and is suitable for heavier lined curtains, which should be 2½ times the finished width. Always use metal hooks, which are stronger and last longer. Slot one hook into the loop nearest each edge of the curtain, then at 3" intervals between.

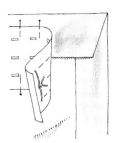
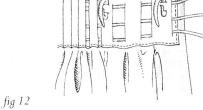

fig 12

sewing on the tape
Leave a heading allowance of 1¼" at the top edge, and press to the wrong side. Press the corners under at a slight angle. Cut the tape to the same measurement as the finished width of the curtain. At one end, knot the cords firmly together on the wrong side and trim. Turn under ⅜" at each end and pin the tape along the top edge, ⅜" down from the fold *(fig 12)*. Stitch in place. Pull up the gathering threads and knot to secure the heading. Do not cut the loose ends – wrap them around a small piece of cardboard and conceal it behind the heading when the curtains are hung.

gathered heading

A ruffled edge can be created simply by stitching the tape farther down from the top of the curtain.

measuring & cutting out
Allow 2½ times the finished width of the curtain and add a heading allowance of twice the desired depth of the ruffle plus ¾" to the finished length.

making the heading
Fold the allowance in half, turning the corners under at a slight angle, and stitch the tape so that it covers the raw edge *(fig 13)*.

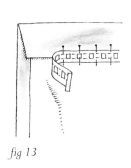
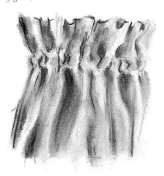

fig 13

buttoned pleats

These hand-stitched box pleats are held in place on the reverse side by flat header tape.

measuring & cutting out
The pleats are made at approximately 6" intervals (distance "a" below). Calculate how many will fit along the finished width of your curtain and add 5" of fabric for each pleat.

making the heading
Fold and pin a series of 5" box pleats (see p.143), leaving distance "a" between them, and baste in place 5" from the top edge. Sew or machine-stitch a length of 1¼" heading tape to the wrong side over the basting line, making sure it is parallel to the top *(fig 14)*. Finish by sewing a button to the front of each pleat. This heading works well on heavyweight unlined fabrics, such as tweed; unravel the threads ¾" along each edge to make a narrow fringe.

fig 14

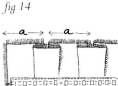
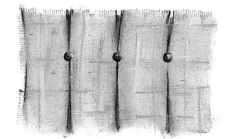

fall-back ruffle

A contrasting piece of fabric sewn along the top of a curtain makes an attractive ruffled heading.

measuring & cutting out

Decide how deep the ruffle should be and cut a strip of fabric twice this width plus 1¼", and the same length as the curtain width. Add a heading allowance of ¾" to the finished length of the curtain.

making

Fold the ruffle piece with right sides together and seam the short ends, making a seam allowance of ⅝". Clip the corners, turn right side out, and press. Sew the header tape ¾" down from the top edge of the curtain. Pin the open edges of the ruffle to the wrong side of the curtain top *(fig 15)* and stitch the two together with a ⅝" seam. Turn the ruffle over to the right side and press the top edge before pulling up the header tape.

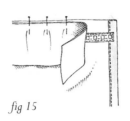

fig 15

valances & swags

Valances and swags provide a decorative frame for the top of a window and can conceal the track or wooden strip below. Depending on how they are sited, they can also give the illusion that a window is taller or wider than it is. Straight or gathered box valances are attached with Velcro to a wooden shelf above the window. A straight valance can be made from a single strip of fabric, or given a decorative chevron edging.

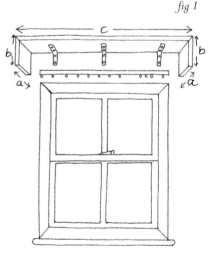

fig 1

gathered box valance

This valance is in effect a short version of the curtains and is usually made to match. Curtain weights can be sewn inside the bottom corners so that it hangs close to the wall. For a lightweight fabric which does not need to be lined, allow an extra half width. Double-hem the sides and lower edge, then follow the method from step 2.

fig 2

making the shelf (fig 1)

Cut the shelf from ¾" plywood and fix to the wall with three or four right-angle brackets. It should be long enough to give 3" clearance at each end of the track (c) and can be 5"–8" wide (a), depending on the size of the window. The side panels are screwed to each end of the board. They help the valance hang straight and keep it clear of the curtains. Cut a strip of Velcro equal to length 2a + c and staple it around the top edge of the shelf *(fig 2)*.

materials

Main fabric, lining fabric, header tape (length = length of finished valance), 1"-wide Velcro strip equal to length of finished valance, wooden valance shelf

measuring & cutting out

Cut main fabric and lining alike: length = 2 x length of finished valance, width = required depth, plus ⅝" seam allowance all around

making

1   Pin the lining and main fabric together with right sides facing and stitch around the sides and lower edge. Clip the corners, turn right side out, and press.

2   Press the seam allowance along the top edge to the wrong side and sew the header tape ⅜" down from the folded edge. Pull it up so that the valance fits exactly around the shelf and knot the cords.

3 Hand stitch the hooked side of the Velcro over the header tape and mount the valance in position.

ruffled valance

This simplest of all valances is mounted directly on the wall. The jaunty ruffle created by the cased heading contrasts particularly well with the straight lines of a swedish shade.

materials

Main fabric, 1"-diameter wooden pole, 2 large screws and anchors, drill and screwdriver

measuring & cutting out

Cut one rectangle: width = 3 x length of pole, length = finished length (from top of frill) + 5"

making

1 Make a ½" double hem along the two sides and the lower edge. Press under a ½" allowance along the upper edge, then fold under a further 4" and press. Pin the fold down and machine stitch a line 1½" down from the top edge. Stitch a second line to hold the folded edge down and to form the casing for the pole.

fig 3

fig 4

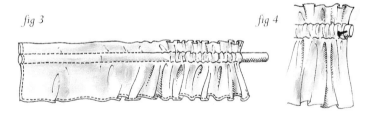

2 Drill a hole ½" from each end of the pole and slide the valance in place on the pole *(fig 3)*. Mark the position on the wall, drill two holes, and insert anchors. Ease back the casing at each end and screw the valance to the wall *(fig 4)*. Pull the loose fabric back to cover the ends of the pole, securing with a few stitches.

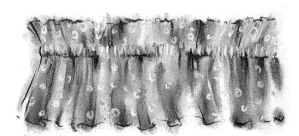

swedish swags

This ingenious method of making swags involves a minimum of sewing, but produces a dramatic effect very quickly. They can be made with or without tails.

materials

Main fabric, 2 small rubber bands, 2 large cup hooks

measuring & cutting out *(figs 5 & 6)*
  – for a swag with tails
Cut one rectangle: length = 2a + b + 2c, width = c, + ¾" hem allowance all around

  – for a swag without tails
Cut one rectangle: length = 2c + b, width = c, + ¾" hem allowance all around

fig 5

fig 6

making

1 Insert the two hooks into the wall above the window at points "d" *(fig 5)*.

2 Make a ½" double hem around all four sides of the fabric. Mark the two points "x" *(fig 6)* as shown. With one hand, pick up the fabric at "x" and bunch it into a point with the other hand *(fig 7)*. Still holding it firmly, slip a rubber band over the point. Do the same at the other end.

3 Slip the bunches over the hooks so that the tails hang down, and adjust so that the swag falls into regular folds.

fig 7

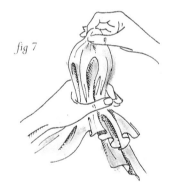

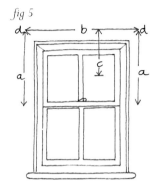

lampshades

There is a great art to making traditional lampshades, but equally effective results can be achieved quickly and simply by dressing up a ready-made shade. Always be sure to use the lightbulb wattage specified for the shade.

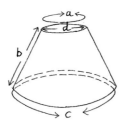

fig 1

handkerchief point lampshade

materials

Lampshade, main fabric, spray adhesive

measuring & cutting out (fig 1)

Shade cover: cut bias strip, width = ½b + 2", length = c + ¾"

Top cover: cut a square, sides = 2b + d + 2¾". Mark and cut out a circle from the center of the square, diameter = d - ¾"

Binding: cut a bias strip, width = 2¾", length = a + ¾"

making

1 With right sides together, join the short ends of the shade cover with a ⅜" plain seam and press open. Spray a light coat of adhesive on the lower half of the lampshade and slip the shade cover over it *(fig 2)*. Smooth the fabric in place. Spray the inside edge of the lampshade and turn under the surplus fabric.

2 Make a ⅜" double hem around the four sides of the top cover. Join the short ends of the binding with right sides together and press open.

3 With right sides together, pin the binding around the edge of the cut-out circle in the top cover. Clip into the curves so they fit neatly, and stitch together ⅜" from the edge *(fig 3)*. Press the seam allowance toward the center. Spray adhesive on the top inside edge of the shade and stick the lower edge of the binding in place, so the handkerchief drapes over the shade.

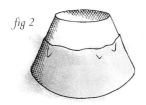

fig 2

fig 3

ruffled lampshade

materials

Lampshade, main fabric, fabric glue

measuring & cutting out (fig 1)

Shade: width = b + 1¼", length = c + 2"

Ruffle: width = 2½", length = 2c

Binding: width = 2", length = a + ¾"

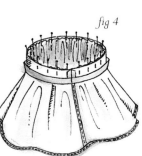

fig 4

making

1 Join the short edges of the binding with a ⅜" plain seam. Press open, then press in half lengthwise. Press under ⅜" around one edge.

2 Join the short edges of the shade with a French seam and double-hem the lower edge. Sew a gathering thread ⅜" from the top and pull up to fit the binding.

3 With right sides together, pin and stitch the gathers to the raw edge of the binding, distributing them evenly *(fig 4)*. Fold the binding along the pressed line and slipstitch to the wrong side.

4 Join the ruffle into a loop and make a narrow double hem along each edge. Gather down the center and pull up to fit around the hem of the shade. Pin, then stitch in place over the gathering line. Remove the gathering thread. Glue top and bottom edges to the shade.

ruched lampshade

materials

Lampshade, main fabric, narrow curtain header tape (length = 1½c + 1½"), spray adhesive, fabric glue

measuring & cutting out (fig 1)

Shade cover: cut a bias strip, width = ½b + 2½", length = c + ¾"

Top cover: width = b + 2", length = 1½c + ¾"

fig 5

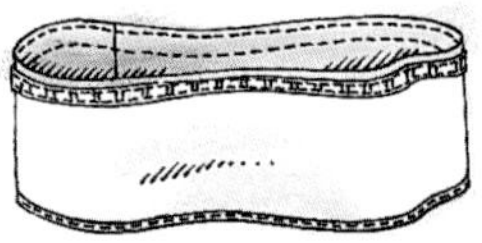

making

1 Cover the shade as for step 1 of the Handkerchief Point Shade.

2 With right sides together, join the two short ends of the top cover. Make a narrow double hem along the lower edge. Press under ¾" along the top edge. Sew header tape to the wrong side, ⅜" from the fold *(fig 5)*. Pull up to fit the shade, and secure.

3 Glue the top cover in place at the top edge. Gather sections of the lower edge and stab-stitch to the shade at various points for a random, ruched effect.

pillowcases

Pillowcases must be easy to put on and take off, and should be made from fabric such as cotton sheeting or linen that will stand up to frequent laundering. Purely decorative pillowcases can be made out of light- to medium-weight fabrics of any description. The European "housewife" cover has an inner flap to hold the pillow in place, and more decorative versions can be made with scallops, ruffles, or contrasting edges.

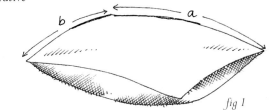

fig 1

basic european "housewife"

materials
Main fabric

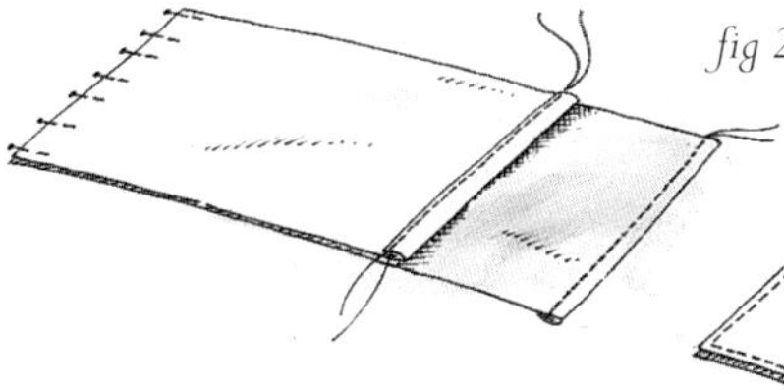

measuring & cutting out (fig 1)
Front: cut one rectangle, length = a + 8", width = b, + ⅝" all around
Back: cut one rectangle, length = a, width = b, + ⅝" all around

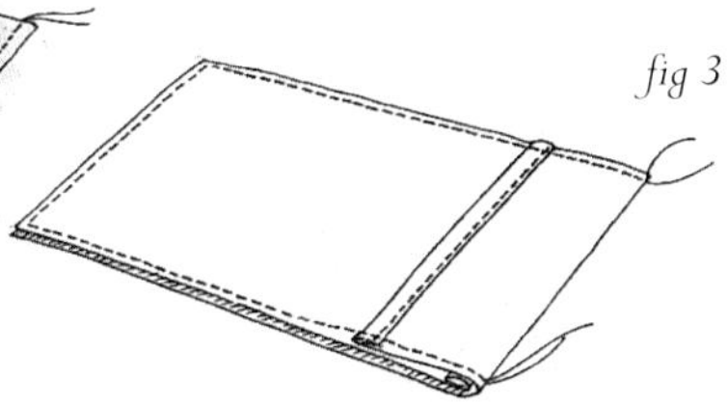

fig 2

fig 3

making

1   Make a narrow double hem at one short end of both pieces. With right sides together, pin the back to the front along the unhemmed ends *(fig 2)*.

2   Fold the flap over so that it lies across the hemmed end of the back piece and pin the two sides together. Stitch around the three unhemmed edges, making a ⅝" seam *(fig 3)*.

3   Trim the seam allowance and zigzag the edges to make the seam more durable. Turn right side out, ease out the corners, and press.

decorative housewife

The contrasting flap lies across the front of the pillowcase and can be trimmed with buttons or a lace edging.

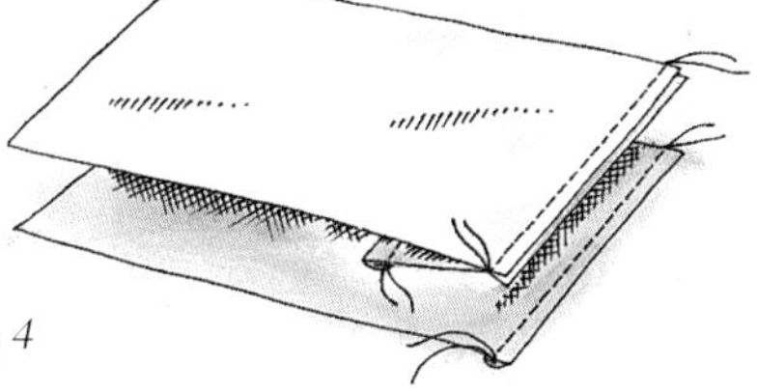

measuring & cutting out (fig 1)
Front and back: cut two rectangles, length = a, width = b, + ⅝" all around
Flap: cut one rectangle, length = 9", width = b, + ⅝" all around

fig 4

making

1   Make a double hem along one short edge of the front piece. Make a narrow double hem along one long edge of the flap.

2   With right sides together, pin the flap to one short edge of the back and stitch along the seam allowance. With right sides together, pin, then stitch the unsewn edges to the front, so that the flap is sandwiched between the two main pieces *(fig 4)*. Finish as for step 3 above.

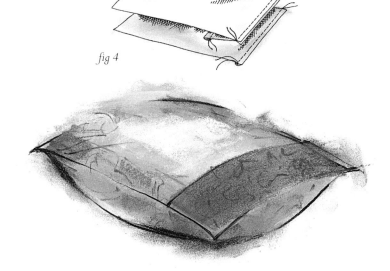

oxford pillowcase

This cover has an integral flap like the Basic European Housewife version, and the flange border is defined by a round of stitching within the outer edge.

materials

Main fabric, ruler, dressmaker's pen or chalk pencil

measuring & cutting out *(see fig 1)*

Front: cut one rectangle, length = a + 12″, width = b, + 5¼″ all around

Back: cut one rectangle, length = a + 2½″, width = b + 5¼″

making

1   Sew a narrow double hem at one short end of each piece. With right sides together, pin the front and back along the unhemmed short edges *(see fig 2)*.

2   Make the flap by folding over the surplus fabric from the front, 2½″ from the hemmed edge of the back piece. Pin the two pieces together *(fig 5)*. Stitch around the three unhemmed edges, making a ⅝″ seam.

3   Turn right side out, ease out the corners, and press. On the right side mark a rectangle 2″ in from the edge using a dressmaker's pen or chalk pencil. Stitch over this line to form the flange *(fig 6)*, but be careful not to catch the open end in the stitching.

scalloped-edge pillowcase

This attractive pillowcase may look complicated to make, but it is simply a variation on the Oxford Pillowcase. To make larger scallops, add extra fabric to the 2″ flange border. A pillow cover can be made in the same way. Cut a square of paper to the finished size and draw on the scallops. Use this as a template for the front and make a vent opening at the back (see p.159).

materials

As for the Oxford Pillowcase, plus large sheet of paper, drawing compass

making

1   Make the pillowcase as in steps 1 and 2 above.

2   Cut a piece of paper the same size as the pillow, plus 2″ all around. Draw a line 2″ in from each edge and using compass, draw a series of semi-circles within this border *(fig 7)*.

3   Pin the paper pattern to the pillowcase and draw around it. Remove and place a pin across each scallop to keep the two layers together, and stitch over the line *(fig 8)*. Clip the curves, trim the seam allowances, turn right side out, and press. On the right side mark a rectangle 2″ in from the edge. Stitch over this line to form the border *(fig 9)*.

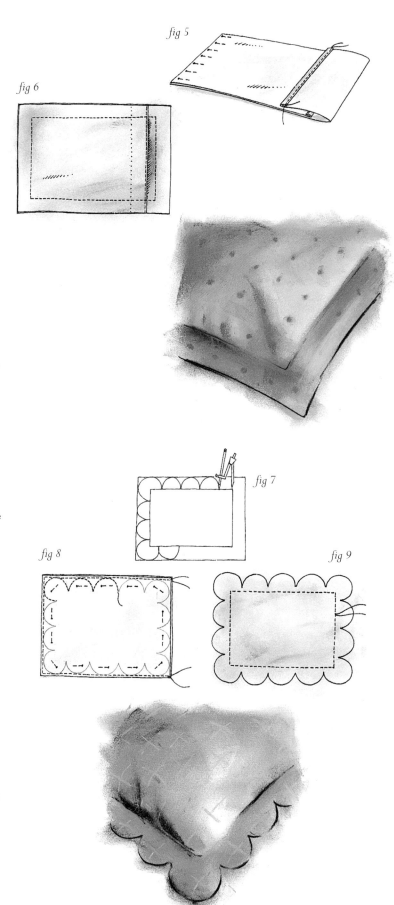

fig 5

fig 6

fig 7

fig 8

fig 9

pillowcase with ruffled edge

A ruffled edge adds an extravagant touch to a plain pillowcase. You can use the same method to make a border from gathered eyelet lace.

materials

Main fabric, ruffle fabric

measuring & cutting out *(see fig 1)*

Front and back: cut two rectangles, length = a, width = b, + ⅝" all around

Flap: cut one rectangle, length = 8", width = b, + ⅝" all around

Ruffle: cut one strip, length = 4 x (a + b), + 2" all around, width = 8"

making

1 Make the double ruffle and attach it to the front piece, making sure the fullness is distributed evenly *(fig 10)*.

2 Sew a 1" double hem along one short edge of the back piece and, with right sides together, pin the other three sides to the front piece *(fig 11)*.

3 Finish one long edge of the flap with a narrow hem. With the right side facing down, pin the unhemmed edges to the open end of the pillowcase *(fig 12)*. Sew around all four sides ⅝" from the edge. Trim and zigzag the seam allowances. Turn right side out and press.

buttoned pillowcase

This open-ended case resembles a large rectangular pillow cover in construction and buttons together along the band. This extra border piece hangs over the edge of the pillow, so that it is not uncomfortable to sleep on.

materials

Main fabric, band fabric, buttons

measuring & cutting out *(see fig 1)*

Main piece: cut one rectangle, width = a, length = 2 x b, + 1¼" all around

Band: cut one strip, width = 12", length = 2 x b, + 1¼" all around

making

1 Press the band in half lengthwise, with wrong sides together. Stitch a ⅜" single hem along one long edge. With right sides together, pin the raw edge of the band to one long edge of the main piece *(fig 13)*. Stitch, making a ⅝" seam.

2 Press the seam toward the band, fold the unit in half crosswise with right sides together. Pin the two raw edges and stitch along the seam *(fig 14)*. Press open the seam on the band. Trim seam allowance on main cover and zigzag edge.

3 Fold the hemmed edge of the band to the wrong side along the crease to conceal the seam below. Pin in place *(fig 15)*. Stitch the band just inside the seam, then turn the cover right side out. You can also topstitch the open edge.

4 Mark the positions for the decorative buttons along the center of the band and make machine buttonholes on the top side of the front band. Sew the buttons to the inside of the back band *(fig 16)*.

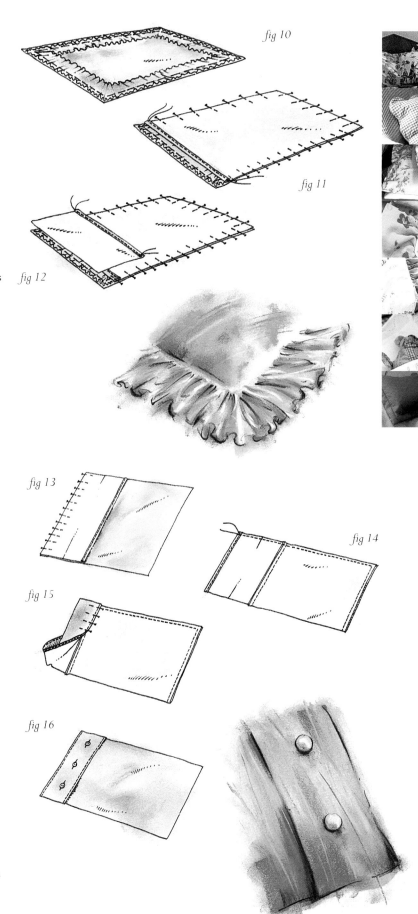

fig 10

fig 11

fig 12

fig 13

fig 14

fig 15

fig 16

pillows

Pillows may be sumptuous, sophisticated, or informal — the variations of shape, size, borders, and trimmings are endless. This section introduces the basic elements — fastenings, fillings, and edgings — that can be put together in any combination to make a highly individual pillow cover.

basic slipstitched cover

The quickest way to close a cover is by hand, with a line of slipstitch. This gives an inconspicuous finish on all fabrics and is the neatest way to finish a piped cover, but the stitches will have to be removed and resewn for cleaning.

materials

Main fabric, pillow form

measuring & cutting out (fig 1)

Front and back: cut two alike, width = a, length = b, or circle with diameter = c, plus ⅝″ all around

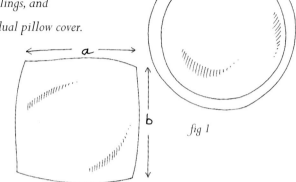

fig 1

making

1   With right sides together pin, then stitch the two pieces together along edge from "d" to "d" *(fig 2)*.

2   Press the seam allowances along the open edge lightly to the wrong side, then clip the corners or curves and turn the cover right side out.

3   Insert the pillow form, easing it into the four corners, and slipstitch the opening neatly together with matching thread *(fig 3)*.

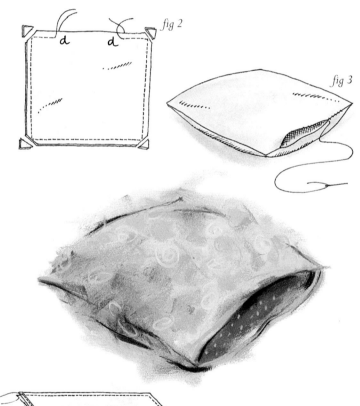

fig 2

fig 3

fastenings

A removable cover must have an opening somewhere. This may be an integral part of the design, as unobtrusive as an envelope backing or as functional as a zipper.

open-ended cover

This slip-on cover looks particularly effective used over a contrasting solid-color pillow and kept in place with ties or bows.

materials

Main fabric, ruler

measuring & cutting out (fig 1)

Front and back: cut two rectangles, width = a + 4½″, length = b + 1¼″

making

1   Sew a narrow double hem along one short end of each piece. With right sides together, pin and stitch around the other three sides, ⅝″ in from the edge *(fig 4)*.

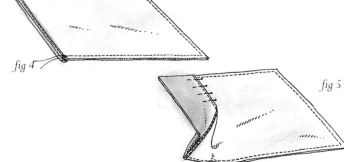

fig 4

fig 5

2 Turn 4″ to the wrong side around the open edge. Check with a ruler that it is even, and press. Pin *(fig 5)*, then stitch in place close to the edge of the hem.

3 If desired, add ties or bows (see p.160).

envelope or vent back

The back is made from two overlapping pieces and the pillow form is slipped between them. This finish can be used on a pillow of any shape and can be made more decorative by adding ties or buttons before assembling.

measuring & cutting out (see fig 1)

For a square cushion:

Front: cut one square, width = a, length = b, + ⅝″ all around

Back: cut two rectangles, width = ½a + 4″, length = b, + ⅝″ all around

For a round cushion:

Front: cut one circle, diameter = c + ⅝″ all around

Back: cut two part circles. To make the template, fold paper pattern for front piece in half along diameter and unfold. Draw a line 4½″ from fold and cut along this line.

making

I Make a narrow double hem along one long edge of each rectangular back piece or along each straight edge for a round pillow.

2 Lay the front piece the right side up, then place one back piece right side down along the right-hand side, matching the outside edge. Place the second piece

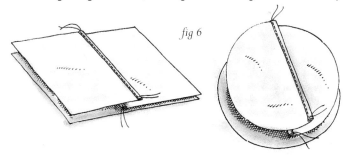

fig 6

to the left so that the hemmed edges overlap *(fig 6)*. Pin and stitch around all sides, making a ⅝″ seam. Clip corners or curves, turn right side out, and press.

zippers

A zipper is the most usual way of fastening a pillow cover that will have a lot of use. It should be 2½″ shorter than the side where it is attached – this may be along the length or across the width depending on the shape. Patterned fabrics should be matched on each side of the opening, and if the fabric has a large-scale repeat it is best to set the zipper close to one side.

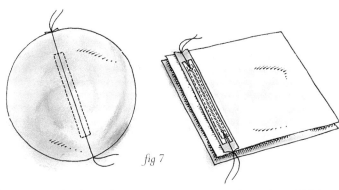

fig 7

There is a special technique for sewing a zipper into a piped seam (see p.144), but for most square or rectangular pillows, it can be placed at the center back. For a round pillow, the zipper should always lie across the center back; it would distort the shape if sewn into the seam *(fig 7)*.

measuring & cutting out (see fig 1)

For a square or rectangular pillow:

Front: cut one piece, width = a, length = b, + ⅝″ all around

Back: cut two pieces, width = ½a , length = b, + ⅝″ all around

For a round pillow:

Front: cut one circle, diameter = c + 1¼″

Back: cut two semicircles, radius = ½c, + ⅝″ all around

making

I With right sides together, pin and baste the two back sections along the seam line. Machine stitch a short seam at each end, leaving a central opening for the zipper. Reverse at the start and finish of the stitching line to reinforce it. Press open and insert the zipper following the instructions (see p. 144).

2 Leaving the zipper partly open, pin the back to the front with right sides together and stitch all around the outside edge, making a seam of ⅝″ all around. Clip the corners or the curves. Turn right side out and press, then insert the form.

pillow forms

Ready-made forms – square, round, and bolster-shaped – are available in many sizes. They are stuffed with feathers, which are soft and long-lasting, or hypoallergenic synthetic polyester, which has the advantage of being fully washable. You can, where necessary, make a specially-shaped form from muslin and stuff it with fiberfill.

edgings

There are many edgings that can be used to embellish a plain square or round pillow. Some, such as gathered or pleated ruffles, piping, and some ready-made fringes, are sewn between the front and back pieces as the cover is being assembled, but others – cord and braid – are sewn by hand to the completed cover (see p.141-3).

piping

Piping cord can be covered in fabric that matches or contrasts with the main cover. Make a length equal to the perimeter plus 2″, and baste in place on the right side of the front piece so that the final seam lies in the center of one edge. Clip the corners for a square; for a circle clip into the seam allowance all around *(fig 8)*. With right sides together, pin and stitch the back piece (or pieces) in position, using a zipper foot to sew close to the stitching.

fig 8

ruffles

Ruffles can have a hemmed or bound edge (see p.142), but the extra fabric in a reversible double ruffle gives the most effective finish. A wide ruffle measuring up to 4″ for a large pillow or 2″ for a smaller one looks even more extravagant. For a full effect, allow twice the perimeter of the pillow form, joining the fabric as necessary and pressing the seams flat. The same measurements and method are used for both square and round covers.

making

1 Pin the ruffle to the seam allowance on the front piece *(fig 9)*, following the technique (see p.142) to make sure the gathers are equally distributed. For a ruffled and piped cushion, first apply the piping, then add the ruffle, remembering to use a zipper foot to sew close to the piping. Baste the ruffle along the seam line, using small stitches to keep it secure. Pin the gathers to the cover front so they do not get caught in the seam.

2 Place the back piece face down on the front and pin, then baste in place. Machine-stitch along the seam allowance, curving gently around the square corners. Clip the corners, turn right side out, and press.

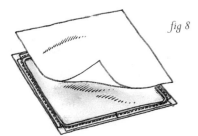

fig 9

decorative fastenings

A slip-on cover must be held in place with ties or buttons. These decorative fastenings can also be used to add interest to a simple vent-back pillow cover.

ties

The ties for an open-ended cover can be in matching or contrasting colors, with square or tapered ends. They can be threaded through specially made buttonholes on each side of the opening *(fig 10)* or sewn to the cover *(fig 11)*. See the method on p.144 for details of how to make ties from fabric, or try using woven braid or ribbon tied into bows. Ties for a vent back should be sewn in place before assembling the cover *(fig 12)*.

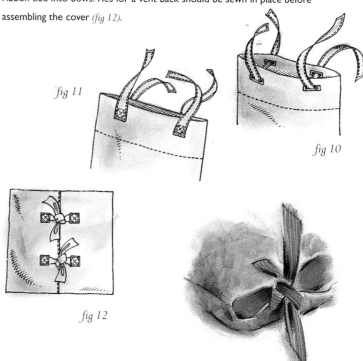

fig 11

fig 10

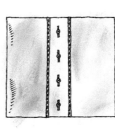

fig 12

buttons

Buttons can also be used to close a slip-on cover *(fig 13)* or to join the two sides of an envelope opening. The top layer of the back could be finished with a placket, like a shirt front *(fig 14)*. Buttons can also be used on the front of a pillow to give a padded, upholstered effect *(fig 15)*, if they are sewn through all layers of the pillow.

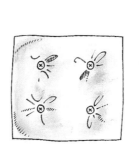

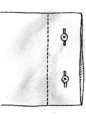

fig 13

fig 14

fig 15

bolsters

Upholstered bolsters have long been used to complement a chaise longue or day bed.
The traditional cover is a tailored cylinder of fabric with piped, flat ends and a zipper, but more decorative
versions have gathered ends trimmed with a button or tassel. Loosely tied ends,
fastened with bows, are even less structured. None of these variations has to
have a zipper – a gathering thread can be temporarily undone if the
cover needs to be removed for cleaning. Omit the seam allowances to
create a really tight-fitting cover. A large bolster for a bed can be made
in the same way by scaling up the fabric requirements.

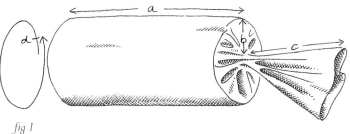

fig 1

tied-end bolster

This informal cover is quick and easy to sew, since it is made from a single length
of fabric.

materials

Main fabric, buttonhole thread, bolster form

measuring & cutting out *(figs 1 & 2)*

Main piece: cut one rectangle: length = a + 2b + 4c, width = d (circumference) +
1¼"

Ties: cut two strips: 2½" x 24"

making

1 With right sides together, sew the two long edges of the main fabric, taking a
⅝" seam. Press the seam open. Make a narrow single hem around each
open end.

2 Using a chalk pencil, mark the two gathering lines (ee) where the ties will go, on
the wrong side of the fabric *(fig 3)*. Turn the surplus fabric at one open edge back
to the wrong side so that the hem lines up with the marked line and baste in
place. Do the same at the other end *(fig 4)*.

3 Turn the cover right side out and sew a round of zigzag gathering
(see p.142) over buttonhole thread on top of each basted line. Insert
the bolster form so that it lies in the middle of the cylinder.

4 Pull up both buttonhole threads tightly to enclose the pad and
tie it securely. Sew the loose ends so that they are hidden inside
the cover *(fig 5)*. The knot can then simply be untied if the cover
has to be removed.

5 Distribute the double gathers evenly to form a rosette shape.
Make the two ties (see p.144) and tie one in a bow at each end,
covering the gathering line.

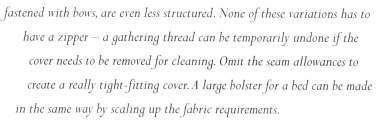

fig 2

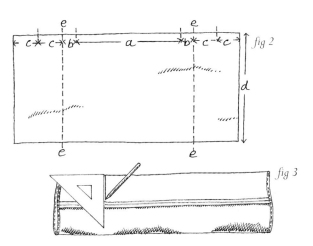

fig 3

fig 4

fig 5

piped bolster with gathered ends

The end pieces can be cut from matching or contrasting fabric, but look particularly dramatic when different textures and patterns are used.

materials

Main fabric, fabric for ends, piping and buttons, bolster form, 2 self-cover buttons, piping cord, button thread

measuring & cutting out (see fig 1 & fig 6)

Main piece: cut one piece: width = a, length (of circumference) = d + ⅝" all around

End pieces: cut two pieces: length (of circumference) = d + 1¼", width = b + 1"

Piping cord and bias strip to cover: length = 2d + 4"

Buttons: cut two circles using the template supplied with the buttons

making

1   With right sides together, stitch the main piece along "a" to make a cylinder, making a ⅝" seam. Press seam open and turn right side out.

2   Cut the piping cord in half and cover it. At each open end of the main piece, pin a round of piping (see p.141) along the seamline, with the cut edges together and the seams matching. Stitch in place using a zipper foot *(fig 7)*.

3   With right sides together, pin the short edges of one end piece to form a loop. Stitch together, making a ⅝" seam and press open. Press ⅜" to the wrong side around one edge. On the right side, make a zigzag gathering line close to the pressed edge (see p.142).

4   With right sides together, pin, then baste the cut edge to one end of the main piece *(fig 8)*, matching the seams. Sew in place, using a zipper foot so that the stitching lies close to the piping. Do the same at the other end.

5   Insert the bolster pad and pull up the gathering thread tightly *(fig 9)*. Tie and sew the loose ends back inside the cover. Cover the buttons and sew on securely so that they conceal the gathered ends *(fig 10)*.

variations

For a more extravagant look, the ends can be made so that they are either gathered more fully or pleated. To do this, make the length of the strips twice the bolster's circumference. Make the main part of the cover as for steps 1 and 2, then continue as follows.

gathered end with extra fullness

3   Stitch the short edges of one end piece to form a large loop, with right sides together. Press open. Fold in half, then half again, and mark the four creases with notches along one edge. On the right side, work four separate zigzag gathers (see p.142) between the notches, stitching close to the edge. Make a continuous zigzag gather around the other edge *(fig 11)*.

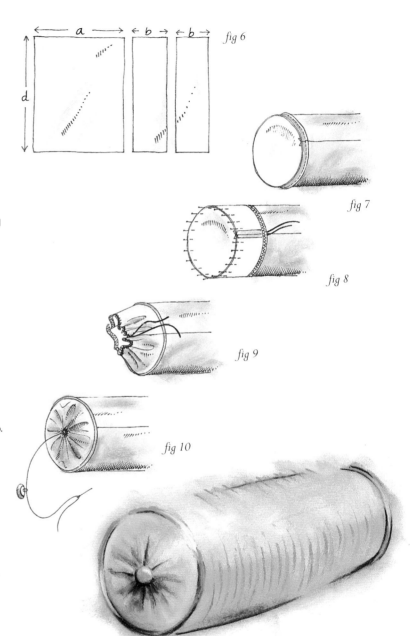

fig 6

fig 7

fig 8

fig 9

fig 10

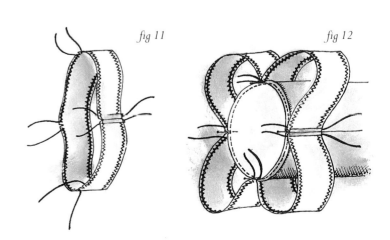

fig 11

fig 12

4 Mark quarter sections on the main cover in the same way. With right sides together, pin, matching the notches *(fig 12)*. Pull up the four gathering threads so that the ring of fabric fits the form tightly, then knot the ends. Pin the gathers, distributing them evenly *(fig 13)* and stitch close to the piping, using a zipper foot. Do the same with the other end and finish as in step 5, left.

pleated end

3 With right sides together, stitch the short edges of one end piece to form a large loop and press open. On the right side, make a line of zigzag gathering, ¼" in from one edge (see p.142). Divide the unstitched edge of the loop and one end of the cover into quarters as in step 3 left. With right sides together, pin the loose fabric in place in a series of narrow, even pleats *(fig 14)*. Baste in place, then stitch close to the piping using a zipper foot. Do the same with the other end and finish as for step 5, left.

flat-ended bolster

This close-fitting cover is fastened with a zipper. It can be trimmed with braid, cord, or fringe, or finished with a round of piping at each end.

material

Main fabric, bolster form, zipper (2½" shorter than length of bolster), braid

measuring & cutting out (see *fig 1* & *fig 15*)

Main piece: cut one rectangle: width = a + 1¼", length = d (circumference) + 1½"

End pieces: cut two circles: diameter = 2b + ⅝" all around

Braid: length = 2d + 1½"

making

1 Insert the zipper (see p.144) so it is centered along the "a" seam of the main fabric *(fig 16)*. Leave the zipper partly open while putting the cover together. Clip ⅜" into the seam allowance around each raw edge at 1¼" intervals.

2 For a piped end only, pin and sew a notched round of piping (see p.141) to the right side of each flat end before sewing the ends in place *(fig 17)*.

3 Make ⅜" notches around the edge of each round end piece, snipping every 1¼". With right sides together, pin, then baste the ends to the main cover. Stitch in place, making a ⅝" seam *(fig 18)*. Press lightly and turn right side out.

4 If trimming with braid, cord, or fringe, cut the trim in two and slipstitch it in place around each edge using a matching sewing thread. Turn the braid under ⅜" at each end and butt the folded edges together. Join them with slipstitch *(fig 19)*. Trim the other end of the bolster in the same way.

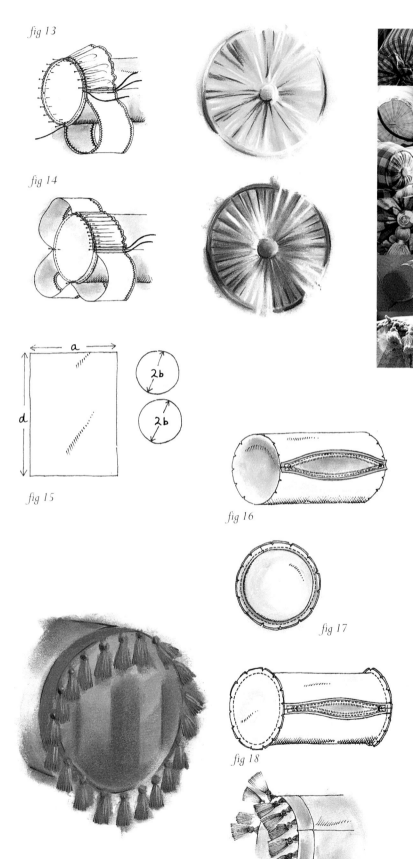

fig 13

fig 14

fig 15

fig 16

fig 17

fig 18

fig 19

cushions *for seating*

Cushions add style, fun, color and comfort to all forms of seating — armchairs, footstools, dining chairs, and benches — and can be made to suit your individual requirements. A cover which will undergo heavy use should be easily removable and made from hard-wearing fabric, without piping or intricate trimmings, while a decorative squab for an antique chair may be more ornate and fragile.

Ready-made forms can be adapted for seating, but upholstery foam is used for fitted or box cushions. Thin foam can be cut with long-bladed scissors, but the deeper type has to be ordered and cut to size. All foam or sponge fillings must conform to current safety regulations. For protection and to give a smooth finish to the finished cushion, the form should first be covered with a close-fitting cotton lining. Make this by following the technique for the finished cover and slipstitch it in place.

gathered-corner cover

This is the simplest method of giving depth to a cover for a square or rectangular form with a soft filling. Add sturdy fabric ties to hold the cushion in place on a chair seat or back.

materials

Main fabric, ruler, tailor's chalk or dressmaker's pen, zipper (4″ shorter than length of cushion form), cushion form

fig 1

fig 2

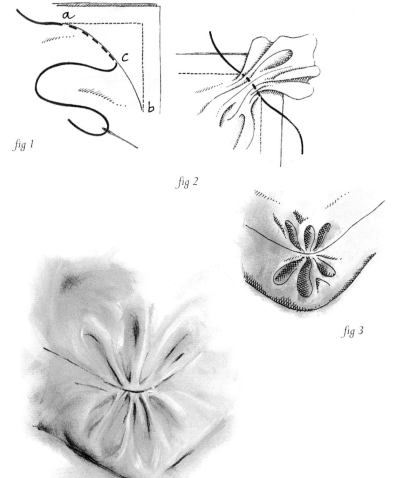

fig 3

measuring & cutting out

Front: cut one piece: same size as cushion, + 1″ all around

Back: cut one piece: width = width of front, length = length of front + 1½″ for zipper

making up

1 Cut the back into two pieces lengthwise and insert zipper (see p.144). With right sides together and zipper open, stitch the front to the back, ⅝″ from the edge.

2 Draw the gathering line at each corner. Mark three points: one 2″ in from the end of each seam (a & b) and one which lies 1″ diagonally in from the corner (c). Join the marks with a shallow curve *(fig 1)*. These measurements can be scaled up for a larger cushion.

3 Using a strong thread, hand-sew along this line and pull up the gathers *(fig 2)*. Wrap the thread around the gathered point and secure the ends. Repeat for each corner. Turn right side out and insert the pad, easing the cover smoothly over the corners *(fig 3)*. To tie the cushion to the back or seat of the chair, make and securely sew two ties at each corner of one side seam (see p.144).

variation

A stylish upholstered look can be given to the finished cushion by attaching either 4″ circles cut from matching fabric or self-cover buttons sewn on through all layers (see *fig 2* on page 121).

fitted box cushion

Deep box cushions are ideal for window seats or day beds, but the same method can be used to make smaller versions to fit chairs and stools. The close-fitting cover is piped around the top and bottom to strengthen the seams and is fastened with a long zipper which extends around the back corners.

materials

Foam cushion form covered with cotton slipcover, main fabric for cover and piping, heavy-duty zipper (length of form plus 6″), piping cord (length = 2 x perimeter of cushion + 4″)

measuring & cutting out (fig 4)

Top and bottom: cut two pieces, width = a, length = b, + ⅝″ all around

Front gusset: cut one piece, width = a, length = c, + ⅝″ all around

Side gussets: cut two, width = b - 4″, length = c, + ⅝″ all around

Back gusset: cut one, length (d) = a + 8″, width = c + 1½″, + ⅝″ all around

making

1 Cut the back gusset in half lengthwise. Following the method on p.144, stitch the zipper in place between the two pieces at "d".

2 With right sides together, pin the narrow ends of the front, side and back gusset pieces together to form a loop. Slip over the pad to check the fit and adjust if necessary. Baste, then machine-stitch the seams, leaving ⅝″ unsewn at each end of the two front seams (*fig 5*). Press the seams open.

3 Attach a round of piping to the outside edge of the top and bottom pieces (see p.141). Clip into the seam allowance of the piping at each corner (*fig 6*).

4 With right sides together, pin the gusset around the bottom piece, matching the front seams to the corners. Clip down to the seam at the back corners (*fig 7*). Baste, then stitch the seam, using a zipper foot to sew close to the piping. Make an extra row of reinforcing stitches at each corner. Open the zipper and attach the piped top piece in the same way, clipping the back corners first (*fig 8*).

5 Trim the seam allowance to ⅜″ and zigzag the raw edges to finish and strengthen. Turn the cover right side out, easing the corners into shape. Insert the form, making sure the seam allowances lie toward the gusset, and close the zipper.

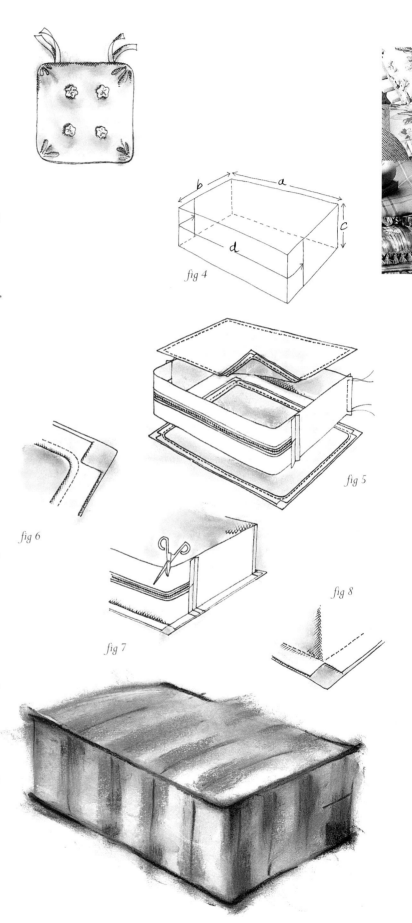

fig 4

fig 5

fig 6

fig 7

fig 8

fitted squabs

A squab cushion is cut to match the shape of a particular piece of furniture. It may be a feather-filled cushion which sits on a stool or in a favorite armchair, or it may be tied on to an upright dining chair. The first step in making any fitted squab is to draw an accurate template of the seat.

footstool squab

materials

Pencil and paper, masking tape, upholstery foam 1½″ deep, marker pen, cotton lining fabric, main fabric, cord (length = perimeter of seat top + 2″)

making the template (fig 9)

Tape a sheet of paper over the stool and smooth it down to reveal the shape of the top. Draw over this edge with a pencil, remove the paper from the stool, and cut along the line. Lay the template back on the stool to check for accuracy.

measuring & cutting out

Lining: cut two pieces the same shape as the template + 1″ all around

Top and bottom: cut two pieces the same shape as the template + 1½″ all around

Form: cut one piece the exact shape of the template

making

1   Pin, then stitch the two lining pieces together, leaving an opening along one straight edge (aa) to insert the pad *(fig 10)*. Clip the curves and trim the seam allowance. Turn right side out, and put the foam in place, and slipstitch *(fig 11)*.

2   Join the main pieces together *(fig 10)*. Clip the curves, turn right side out, and insert the covered form. Slipstitch the opening, leaving a gap of ¾″. Attach the cord, following the method on p.141, concealing the ends inside the gap.

ruffled cushion for a basket chair

A basket chair requires a special cushion pad. This can easily be made from cotton lining or muslin, cut to the shape of the seat (make a paper template as above). The plumper the cushion, the more luxurious it will appear, so stuff the pad well.

materials

Fiberfill, cotton lining fabric, main fabric

measuring & cutting out

Lining: cut two pieces the same size as the template, + ⅝″ all around

Front and back: cut two pieces the same size as the template, + 1″ all around

Ruffle: cut one strip, 10″ wide by 2 x straight edge of cushion

making the cushion pad

1   Pin and stitch the two pieces of lining fabric together with a seam allowance of

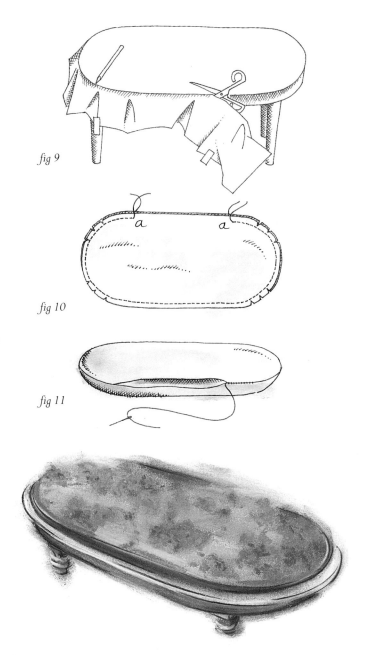

fig 9

fig 10

fig 11

½″, leaving a 4″ opening along the straight edge. Clip the curves. Turn right side out, stuff firmly with fiberfill and slipstitch the opening securely.

making the cover

2   With right sides together, fold the ruffle in half lengthwise. Stitch together the two sides of each short end. Clip the corners, turn right side out, and press, then stitch along the raw edges to secure.

3   Place the cushion top right side up. Pin one end of the ruffle to each front corner, ⅝″ in from the sides, with the folded edge lying inward. Arrange the fullness into evenly spaced box pleats (see p.143) and pin in place *(fig 12)*. Stitch in place ⅝″ from the edge.

4 Press under the seam allowance along the straight edge of the back piece. Pin the front and back together with right sides together. Sew around the outside seam line, taking care not to stitch into the ruffle. Clip the curves, turn right side out, and press. Insert the form and slipstitch the folded edge of the back to the ruffle along the stitched line *(fig 13)*.

tie-on squab

The method for cutting a template for an upright chair is slightly more complicated, as it has to fit around the struts, but the technique is the same as for the stool. This version is piped, but alternative finishes include a gathered ruffle or sew-on braid or fringe. A zipper could be inserted along the back seam if necessary, but a slipstitched opening can easily be undone if the cover needs to be washed.

materials

Pencil and paper, masking tape, upholstery foam (1½″ deep), cotton lining fabric, main fabric, covered piping cord to fit perimeter of seat top + 2″

making the template (fig 14)

Smooth the paper over the seat to reveal the underlying shape. Snip around the struts and tape the paper in place securely. Draw around the outline and fold the paper in half. Cut out around the pencil line, then check against the seat. Mark the position of the ties on each side of the struts.

measuring & cutting out

Pad: cut one piece the exact shape of template

Lining: cut two pieces the same size as the template, + 1″ all around

Back and front: cut two pieces the same size as the template, + 1⅜″ all around

Ties: cut four strips, 2½″ x 15″

making

1 Make the inner cover by sewing the two lining pieces together along the sides and front from "b" to "b" *(fig 15)*, making a ⅝″ seam. Clip the corners and turn right side out. Insert the form and slipstitch the opening.

2 Transfer the tie position marks ("a" and "b") to the main back piece. Sew a line of reinforcing stitches along the seam line from "a" to "b" at the corners of both the front and back pieces. Clip the seam allowance around the curves and corners. Make the ties (see p.144) and pin, then stitch them to the back piece *(fig 15)*.

3 Attach the covered piping to the main front piece *(fig 16)* so the seam lies at the center back (see p.141). With right sides facing, stitch the front and back pieces together along the curved edges of the sides and front, using a zipper foot to sew close to the piping. Turn under and press the unstitched seam allowance on the back piece. Insert the pad and slipstitch the opening from "b" to "b" along the underside of the piping *(fig 17)*.

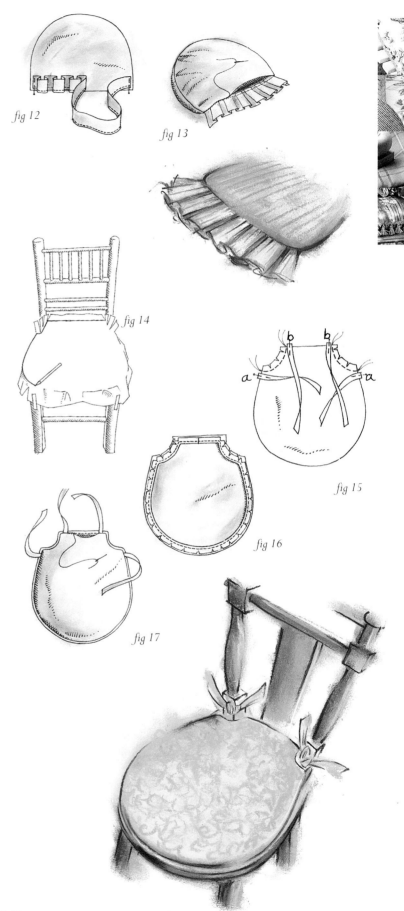

fig 12

fig 13

fig 14

fig 15

fig 16

fig 17

slipcovers

Slipcovers serve several purposes — they can protect upholstery, disguise a worn but comfortable armchair, or provide an effective update for an old wooden chair. All chairs vary in shape and proportion, so careful measurement is essential for a professional finish. When making a cover, you should start with a muslin toile or preliminary version. Like a couturier designing a one-of-a-kind garment, you can adjust this on the chair itself to achieve a perfect fit before cutting out the main fabric.

two-piece chair cover

This set is designed for a straight-backed dining chair; the fitted seat cover and separate back can be made in any combination of fabrics and skirt lengths. The seat is held in place with either a cross-over tie or two bows.

materials

Paper, pencil, masking tape, main fabric, cotton lining fabric

measuring & cutting out (figs 1, 2, & 3)

Measure your chair and decide on the proportions: depth of the back (b) and ruffle (c) (3"-4"), skirt length (from 4"-12"), and the width and number of ties. Add a seam allowance of ⅝" all around each piece.

Seat: make a template *(fig 2)*. Add an extra 2" to "f" and "e," shown by the shaded area. Cut two, one from main fabric and one from lining

Front skirt: cut one, width = 4e + 2f + 6", depth = g

Back skirt: cut one, width = 2d, depth = g

Ties: cut two or four, length = 30", width (y) = 4"-7"

Back: cut two, width = a + (z) 2"-3", depending on the thickness of chair, depth = b (half the height of the back)

Ruffle: cut one, width = 4a, depth = 2c. Notch the center of one long side

making the seat cover

1 Make a ⅜" double hem (equal turns) along the side and bottom edges of the two skirt pieces. With right sides together, pin the top corners of the back skirt to the seat back (along d), ⅝" from the edges. Fold the skirt into knife pleats (see p.143), 1½" apart, along the unhemmed edge. Pin them in place as you go, then stitch down, ⅝" from the edge.

2 With right sides together, pin the top corners of the front skirt to the sides of the seat, ⅝" down from the curves. Pin into equal pleats, making sure that the last fold at each corner lies ⅝" from the adjacent side *(fig 4)*. Stitch together, clipping into the seam allowance of the skirt *(fig 5)*.

3 Make the ties as on p.144. Pin, wrong sides up, at points "a" for a single tie and "a" and "b" for a double bow *(fig 6)*. Turn the ties back into the center of the seat cover with right sides together, pin the lining to the seat, checking that the skirts and ties are not caught up.

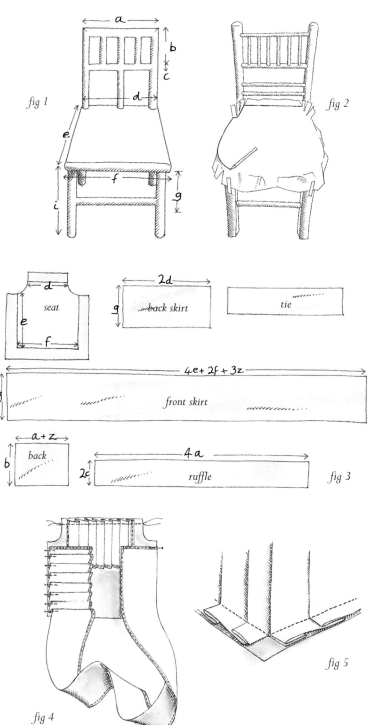

fig 1

fig 2

seat

back skirt

tie

front skirt

back

ruffle

fig 3

fig 4

fig 5

4 Stitch together around the outside edge from "b" (inner edge of tie) to "b." Keep the main fabric uppermost and sew over the existing seam. Double stitch the corners and ties. Clip the corners and turn right side out. Press under and slipstitch the top edge of the lining.

making the chair back

5 With right sides together, pin and stitch the two pieces together around the sides and top, ⅜″ from the edge. Turn right side out and press. Join the short ends of the ruffle with right sides together and press the seam open. With wrong sides together, fold in half lengthwise and press.

6 Match the seam and notch on the ruffle to the side seams on the chair back cover and pin. Fold, pin, and stitch the ruffle into pleats all around the opening *(fig 7)*. Press the seam allowances in, and finish with a line of topstitching, ⅛″ above the seam.

box-pleated seat cover

This long-skirted variation is ideal for firmer fabrics such as wool plaids which would be too stiff for gathers. A solid-backed chair does not require a back skirt.

materials

Main fabric, lining fabric

measuring & cutting out

Seat: cut two, one from main fabric and one from lining. Notch the center front and center sides

Front skirt: cut one, length = 2e + f + 20″, width = approx 8″. Notch the center top edge

Ties: cut four, length = 2″, width = 12″

making

Make a ⅜″ double hem (equal turns) along the side and bottom edges of the skirt. Fold a ¾″ pleat on each side of the notch, and with right sides together, pin to the center front of the seat. Do the same at the corners and center of each side. Fold under the surplus fabric at each edge so that it lies ⅜″ in from the curve *(fig 8)*. Stitch along the seam allowance, clipping at the corners (see *fig 5* left). Complete as for steps 3 and 4 above.

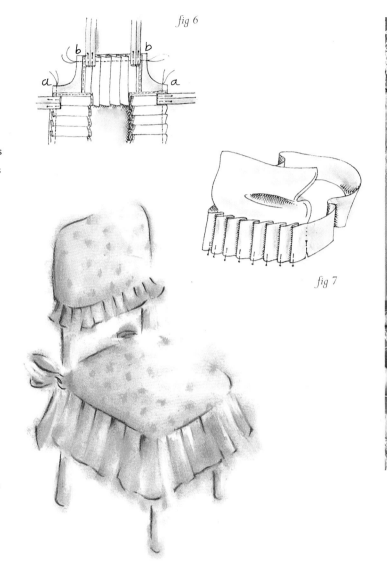

fig 6

fig 7

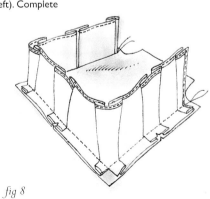

fig 8

flounced cover

The feminine flounces of this cover, designed for a chair with a round seat, recall a lavish silk ballgown. It has a full, gathered skirt trimmed with braid, and the back is decorated with a sash and luxurious long-tailed bow.

materials

Paper, pencil, masking tape, main fabric, sash and bow fabric, covered piping cord (length = a + 2b + d + 2″), 20″ zipper, 1 large snap fastener (optional), braid (length = 2c + 2d), button thread for gathering

measuring & cutting out (figs 9 & 10)

Measure your chair, noting the shape and thickness of the back. If the top edge is the same width or narrower than the bottom edge, the cover will slip easily over the chair and you can omit the zipper. Make a muslin toile of the back and seat; it may be necessary to cut the inside back slightly smaller than the outside to get the best fit. Add ⅝″ around each piece for the seam allowance. Make a template for the seat (see *fig 2* on page 168).

Inside and outside back: cut two, top width = a + 2″ (depending on thickness), bottom width = c, height = b

Seat: cut one, as template

Skirt: cut one, width = e (highest point of top edge of seat to floor), length = 2c + 2d

Sash: cut two, length = ½c + 2″, width = 10″

Bow: Main part: cut one, width = 32″, length = 16″

      Center: cut one, width = 4″, length = 8″

      Tails: cut two, width = 18″, length = 8″

making

1 With right sides together, pin and stitch the back of the seat to bottom of inside back, making a ⅝″ seam. On the right side attach a round of piping to outside edge (see p.141). Clip the seam allowance of the piping cover at regular intervals.

2 Fold one of the sash pieces in half lengthwise with right sides facing and join the long edges together. Turn right side out and press flat, so that the seam lies at center. Fold the seam allowance at one end to the inside and sew a gathering thread through both finished edges. Pull up and fasten securely *(fig 11)*. Make the other sash, gathering the opposite end to make a pair.

3 With right sides together, pin and stitch one ungathered end of the sash to each side of the inside back, so that the lower edges lie on the seam line *(fig 12)*.

4 Pin the outside back to the inside back with right sides together. Stitch around the sides and top, using a zipper foot to sew close to the piping. Leave ⅝″ unstitched at the lower edge. If you are adding a zipper, leave 12″ open on the right-hand edge *(fig 13)*.

5 Stitch the short edges of the skirt with right sides together. Leave the top 9″ of the seam open for the end of the zipper. Make a zigzag gather (see p.142) ⅝″ down from the top edge, starting and finishing ⅝″ in from the edges. Pull up the cord to half its length.

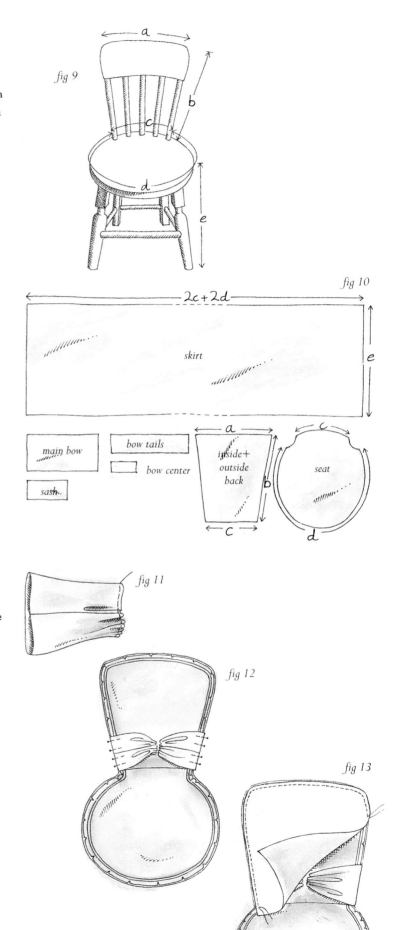

fig 9

fig 10

fig 11

fig 12

fig 13

6 Slip the back and seat onto the chair, wrong side out. Pin the skirt to the outside back and seat edge, lining up the seam or opening with the right-hand edge of the back, and distribute the gathers evenly *(fig 14)*. Remove from the chair and stitch in place using a zipper foot, and sewing close to the piping on the seat. Insert the zipper at this stage, following the instructions on p.144. Clip the curves, turn right side out, and press lightly.

7 Make the bow as on p.144. Stitch the gathered end of the right-hand sash to the center back seam and stitch the bow securely on top. Sew one half of the snap to the end of the left-hand sash and the other half under the bow, close to the center *(fig 15)*. If there is no zipper, sew both ends of sash to the cover.

8 Put the cover on the chair, then turn up the hem level with the floor and finish. Sew braid around the hem.

pleated cover

This elegant variation is assembled in exactly the same way, but without the sash. Its skirt is box-pleated instead of gathered, and the seams are not piped, but concealed with gold braid, sewn on by hand once the cover is complete. Measure around the seat and the top edge of the back to find out how much braid is needed.

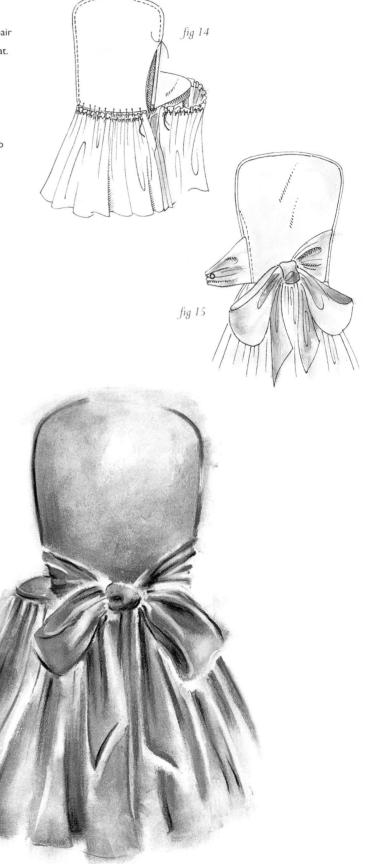

fig 14

fig 15

tailored cover

The boxy lines of this cover are intended for an upright dining chair with a square seat. It looks particularly effective when made in checks, plaid, or stripes. The optional side pockets are a useful place to store a book or magazine.

materials

Main fabric

measuring & cutting out (figs 16 & 17)

The shaded areas indicate a seat or back which is wider at the top or bottom edge and the broken lines represent fold lines. The 4″ skirt pleats should allow the cover to fit most chairs, but if the legs are very splayed, calculate the extra amount needed and add one eighth of this to each pleat. Add ⅝″ all around each piece. NB: z equals 2″ in the cutting instructions below.

Inside back: cut one, top width = a + z (depending on thickness), bottom width = d, depth = h. Notch the center top edge

Seat: cut one, top width = d, bottom width = f, side depth = e

Front skirt: cut one, width = f + 4z, depth = i. Notch fold lines at top and hem

Side skirt: the back legs may be a different height from the front legs; measure "i" and "j" carefully, so that the skirt hangs straight.

Cut two, width = e + 4z, height at one edge = i, the other j. Notch fold lines at top and hem

Pockets: make a rectangular template to fit onto the side skirt.

Cut two, as template

Outside back: add 2″ or more to "a", depending on thickness of back. If you are working with stripes or plaids, add extra fabric so that the box pleat folds along the pattern lines, and alter the center 8″ pleat allowance accordingly.

Cut one, as pattern. Notch the center top and the fold lines at top and hem.

Ties: cut six, width = 2″, length = 14″ including seam allowance

making

1 Make the box pleat on the right side of the outside back by lining up the fold lines at top and bottom, and turning to the center. Press well for a sharp crease. Pin in place along top edge, then stitch down, ⅜″ from the edge *(fig 18)*.

2 Sew a ⅜″ double hem at the top of each pocket. Press under the seam allowance on the other sides. Pin one to each side skirt and topstitch down.

3 With right sides together, pin and stitch together the side and front skirts, matching the edges of pleats "i." Join the edge of pleats "j" to the outside back *(fig 19)*. Make the corner pleats "i" by matching the notches. Pin at the top and bottom edges and fold toward the middle. Press well. Stitch together along the top edge to hold in place. Do the same with the back pleats "j" *(fig 20)*.

4 Pin the inside back to the outside back with right sides together. Stitch around the sides and top, ⅜″ from the edge, leaving the seam allowance on the lower edge unstitched. With right sides together, pin and stitch the top edge of the seat to the lower edge of the inside back.

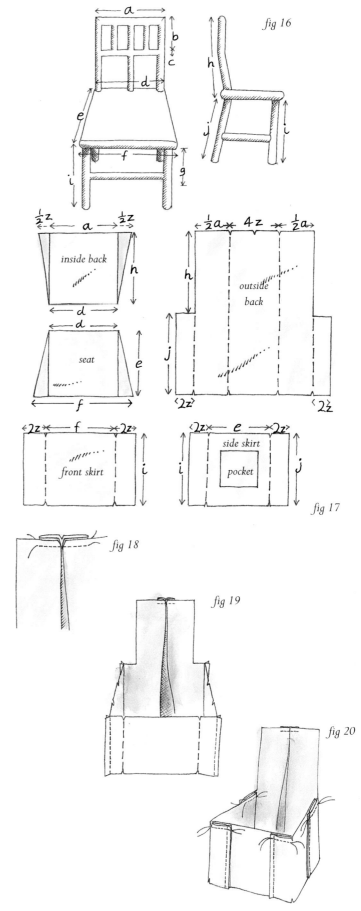

fig 16

fig 17

fig 18

fig 19

fig 20

5 Pin the top edge of the skirt to the sides and lower edge of the seat, making sure the pleats are in position. Stitch along the seam allowance, reinforcing the corners.

6 Turn right side out. Check that the lower edge is level, then finish and turn up the hem. Make the ties as on p.144 and sew in pairs to the inner edges of the box pleat at 6″ intervals.

basket chair cover

This deceptively sophisticated cover is designed to go over a traditional Lloyd Loom chair, but could easily be adapted for any tub-shaped armchair or wicker seat. It is skillfully cut, in just five main pieces, with box pleats at the back.

materials

Newspaper, marker pen, masking tape, main fabric

measuring & making the pattern (figs 1 & 2)

The seat, sides, and back can be cut out easily, but the inside back piece is more complicated and the shaping has to be accurate. Make a paper pattern first, and if you want to be extra sure, sew a muslin toile before cutting the main fabric. Cut four paper rectangles as indicated in *fig 2*. Tape them to the chair and cut to the exact shape. The shaded areas represent areas that will be cut away and the broken lines are folds. NB: z equals 2″ in the cutting instructions below.

Side: width = $h + z$, depth = $m + n$

Cut away a rectangle ($m \times z$) from the top right corner, to leave the fabric for the box pleat ($n \times z$) at the bottom right edge. Shape the top edge to the outside curve of the arm (d).

Outside back: width = $l + 6z$, depth = $m + n$.

Cut away a rectangle ($m \times 3z$) at each top corner. Shape the top edge to the outside curve of the back (c).

Seat: width = k, depth = $i + f$

Cut the upper part to fit the shape of the chair seat (a).

Inside back: width = $a + 12z$, depth = $b + 3z$ (or more, depending on angle of back) Fold in half crosswise and tape to the center back (b), so that the top of the fold lies on the outside edge. Cut the curve along the outside edge of the back and arm. Mark line "j" (inside front arm). Cut the bottom edge of the pattern into a curve so that it fits around "a", as far as "j." Remove from the chair, and draw a line which continues curve "d" to the edge of the paper. Cut along this line. Retape to the chair, fitting the extended curve to the outside front arm. Fold the surplus paper to fit around the front arm, pinning along "j" *(fig 3)*. Trim the bottom of the front arm so that it continues curve "a." Take the pattern off and cut along the pinned line.

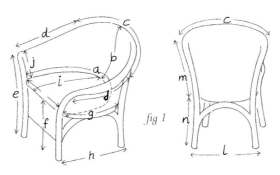

fig 1

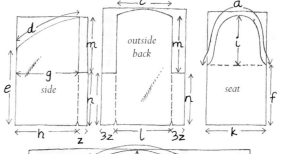

fig 2

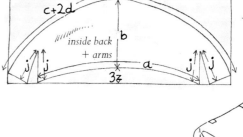

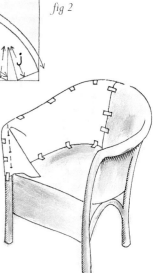

fig 3

cutting out

Add ⅝″ seam allowance around the edge of each pattern piece. Cut out from main fabric:

Sides: cut two

Inside back: cut one. Notch the center of top & bottom edges

Seat: cut one. Notch the center of top curved edge

Outside back: cut one. Notch the center of top edge and fold lines at the hem.

Ties: cut four, 2½″ x 16″

making

I With right sides together, join one side piece to the back at "k" and "j," sewing ⅝″ from the edge. Press the top part of the seam open. Pin the box pleat into place along its top edge *(fig 4)*. Sew across the pleat, ⅜″ from the folds. Do the same with the other side.

2 Join the darts at "l" on the wrong side. Trim the seam allowance to ⅜″ and press toward the outside edge. With right sides together, pin and stitch the curved edge of the seat to the inside back and front arms, matching the notches *(fig 5)*. Trim the seam allowance to ⅜″ and zigzag to finish and strengthen.

3 With right sides together, and matching the notches at center top, pin the back and sides to the seat and inside back. Clip the seam allowance on the inside back at the point where it meets side corners, on the front arm. Stitch along the allowance, then trim back to ⅜″ and zigzag.

4 Fold the pleats, lining up the notches and press well. Make the ties as on p.144 so both ends are squared off. Stitch a pair 2″ from the top edge of each pleat and tie bows *(fig 6)*.

5 Slip the cover onto the chair. Check that the lower edge is level. Finish, and turn up and stitch the hem.

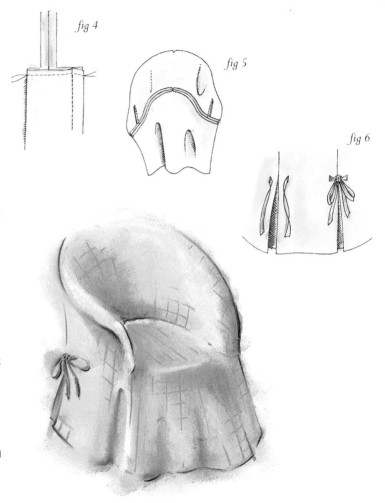

fig 4

fig 5

fig 6

director's chair cover

The folding director's chair is a classic, but this cover gives it a new twist. The skirt is made separately and stitched into box pleats, then sewn to the back, seat, and arms. The opening is concealed down one side.

materials

Main fabric, marker pen, large snap fastener

measuring & cutting out (figs 1 & 2)

Cut the pieces to the measurements for *fig 2*, add an extra 2″ all around. Add an extra 2″ to the back and the left arm, as shown by the dotted lines, where the opening will be. Add an extra 2½″ to the lower edge of the skirt pieces for the hem. Notch all skirt pieces at top and hem to mark the folds, indicated by the broken lines. Now cut the back and arms to shape as shown; the shaded areas represent the fabric to be cut away. NB: z equals 4″ in the cutting instructions opposite.

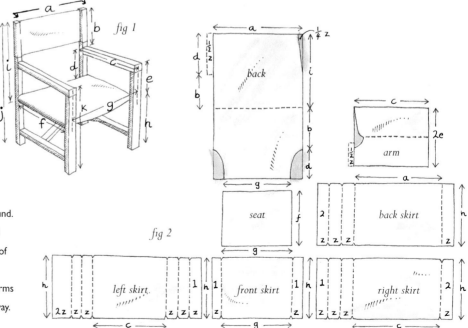

fig 1

fig 2

back

arm

seat

back skirt

left skirt

front skirt

right skirt

Back: cut one, width = a, length = i + b + d. Fold in half crosswise and pin the edges together along the upper part (b). Pin a small box pleat at the fold to accommodate the width of the frame *(fig 3)*

Arm: cut two, width = c (outside edge of back to center front of arm), length = 2e (center top of arm to top of seat). Fold in half crosswise, place over one arm and pin the outside edge to the side of the seat. Pin the inside edges to both sides of the back, following the lines shown, so that the seam lies down the center side of the back strut. Mark along the pinned line, then trim the seam allowance to ⅝"

Seat: cut one, width = g, depth = f

Left skirt: cut one, width = c + 7z, length = h

Right skirt: cut one, width = c + 4z, length = h

Front skirt: cut one, width = g + 2z, length = h

Back skirt: cut one, width = a + 4z, length = h

making

1 Fold the back in half crosswise with right sides together. Pin and sew the top edges together to within ¾" of the fold, 1" from the edge. Make a small box pleat from the unstitched fabric and stitch down, sewing from each side to the center in turn *(fig 3)*. Do the same on the outside arm edges.

2 With right sides together, pin and stitch the back edge of the seat to the bottom edge of the inside back. Join the inside edge of the arms to the lower edges of the back (d), along the seam allowance. Clip the seams where necessary. Sew the outside edge of the right arm to the back. Finish and hem the raw side edge of the left arm. Sew the seat to the bottom edge of the arms *(fig 4)*.

3 Sew the side skirts to the front skirt with right sides together at (1), then join the left side of the back skirt to the side skirt at (2). Hem the two short edges. At the three seams, match the notches and seam lines to make 4" box pleats. Make a single pleat at the right edge of the back skirt *(fig 5)*. Pin in place, and stitch down, ⅝" from the top edge.

4 Pin the top edge of the skirt to the main part with right sides together, so the corners of the front seat and the right back line up to the center of each pleat. Stitch along the seam allowance, reinforcing the corners. Turn right side out and press the pleats, using the notches on the hem as a guide.

5 Put the cover on the chair and check that the skirt is hanging level. Finish the edge and turn up a 2½" hem. Turn the surplus fabric at the left-hand edge of the back skirt to the wrong side and press. Sew the snap fastener to each side of the opening as shown *(fig 6)*.

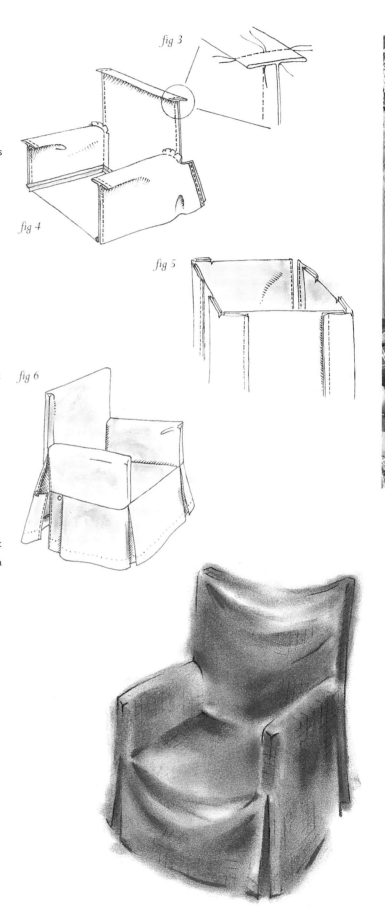

fig 3

fig 4

fig 5

fig 6

director's chair with hood

This variation is much simpler in structure – it does not have a separate skirt – but in a flight of fancy, the back extends to form a long tassel-trimmed hood.

materials

Main fabric, covered piping cord (length = 2k + 2c + distance around edge of hood), large tassel

measuring & cutting out (see figs 1 & 2 on page 174 & fig 7)

Cut the pieces as shown in the diagram. The small curves on the side edges of the outside and inside back pieces allow the cover to fit over the thickness of the arms. Make the measurements for the inside back and inside arm to the outside edges of the arms. Add a ⅝″ seam allowance all around.

making

1 With right sides together, sew the top edge of the seat to the lower edge of the inside back. Sew sides "d" and "f" of the inside arms to the inside back and seat *(fig 8)*.

2 Stitch the outside arms to each side of the outside back, so the curves line up. With right sides together, fold the top edge of the back in half. Pin and stitch to form the hood *(fig 9)*. Do the same with the inner back.

3 Stitch a line of piping (see p.141) around the outside edge of arms and back. With right sides together, pin the inner part of the cover to the outside, and sew together around the arms and back, using a zipper foot. Turn right side out and press. Hem the bottom edge, and sew the tassel to the point of the hood.

bedroom chair cover

This low, armless chair provides a good introduction to the techniques involved in making slipcovers for upholstered furniture, which have to accommodate the thickness of the padding. Extra fabric (tuck-in) also has to be added where the seat and back meet to prevent the cover from straining at the seams during use.

materials

Muslin, tailor's chalk, waterproof marker pen, main fabric, covered piping cord (length = a + 2h + f + 6″), 12″ zipper

measuring & cutting out (figs 1 & 2)

Cut three muslin rectangles for the main pieces, adding 2″ all around and a 6″ tuck-in at the bottom of the inside back and the top of the seat. Label each piece.

Inside back: cut one, width = a, depth = b + tuck-in

Seat: cut one, width = c, depth = d + tuck-in

Outside back: cut one, width = g, depth = h

Ruffle: cut one, length = 2e + 2g, depth = f

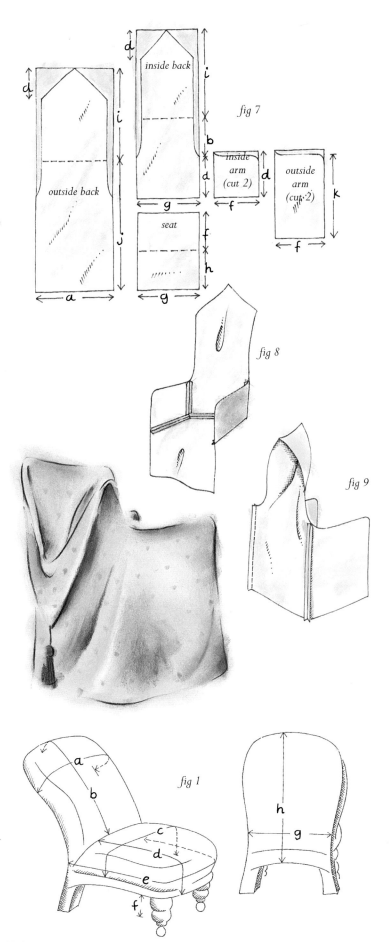

fig 7

fig 8

fig 9

fig 1

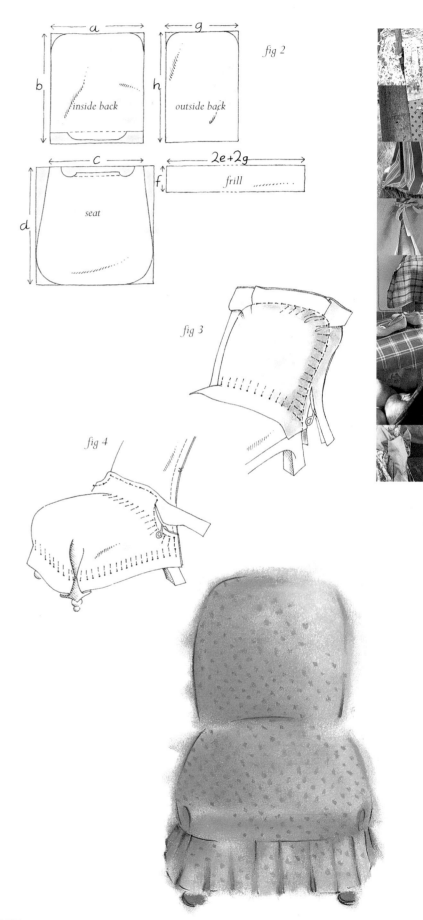

fig 2

inside back

outside back

seat

2e+2g

frill

fig 3

fig 4

cutting the toile

The muslin pieces can be molded to shape on the chair itself, using the seams on the existing upholstery as a guide to pinning them together. They can then be used as a pattern to cut out the main fabric. The shaded areas on *fig 2* show the areas that will be cut away to give the final shape.

1 Chalk a vertical line on the chair to mark the center seat and back. Each piece is folded in half lengthwise, and pinned to this guide line at top and bottom to check that the cover is symmetrical. Smooth the fabric as you work and keep the grain straight. Insert the pins at 4″ intervals at right angles to the seam lines. Pin each piece through the padding to the outside edges of its respective section and to the adjacent pieces in the following order:

a inside back: pin to the outside edge of the chair back, making two pleats at each top corner.

b outside back: pin to the chair back. Inserting the pins in a straight line, pin the two pieces together across the top, then down each side. Trim back the seam allowance to ¾″ *(fig 3)*. Notch the center sides and back, and mark where the pleats lie.

c seat: pin over the side and front edges, making an inverted box pleat to fit the surplus fabric around the front seat corners. Pin the top edge to the outside back and outer edge of the inside back where they meet, along the existing seam lines.

d Fold back the tuck-in on the lower inside back and pin to the tuck-in on the seat. Slip inside the seam and adjust as necessary for a neat fit. Trim back the surplus fabric to ¾″ *(fig 4)*. Notch the center front and sides and mark the front corner pleats. Draw over the pinned lines with a marker pen before separating the sections. Finish the edges, press, and cut out the main fabric.

making the cover

2 Stitch down the pleats at the front corners of the seat and top of the inside back. With right sides together, pin and stitch the top of the seat to the lower edge of the inside back.

3 Sew a line of piping (see p.141) to the sides and top of the outside back. With right sides together, pin and stitch the inside back and top edges of the seat to the outside back using a zipper foot. Leave 12″ unstitched at one lower edge and insert the zipper in this gap (see p.144). Sew the rest of the piping around the lower edge of the cover.

4 Finish the lower edge and sides of the ruffle. Pin around the lower edge of the cover in a series of regular box pleats 2″ apart, and sew in place with a zipper foot. Clip any tight curves and turn right side out. Press.

tie-backed armchair

All armchairs look different, but the basic structure is the same. Although this cover may appear complicated, it consists of just ten pieces which are assembled in a set order. The instructions given are for a tieback cover with a scalloped edge, but it can easily be adapted for a zipped opening and a separate ruffle.

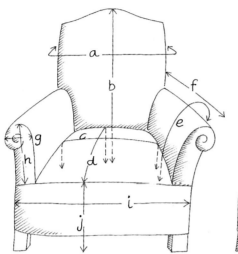

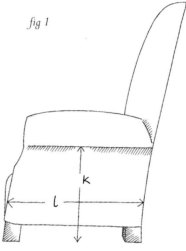

fig 1

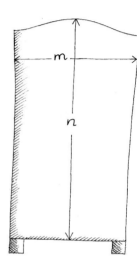

materials

Muslin, tailor's chalk, waterproof marker pen, main fabric, covered piping cord (length = 2g + 4h + i + 2l + 2n + m)

measuring the toile (figs 1 & 2)

Cut seven rectangles from muslin – one for each piece, using *fig 2* as a guide. Make each measurement at the widest point of the section and add 2″ all around. Include 6″ extra tuck-in at the bottom edge of the inside back, inside arms, and the side and back edges of the seat.

cutting the toile

Following the pinning and cutting method for the bedroom chair (p.177), cut each piece to shape. It is only necessary to make the arm cover for one side.

1   Outside back: pin flat to all four side edges of the back, following the shape of the chair. For a back cover with ties, cut the back in two vertically when you eventually unpin the pieces and add an extra 2″ to each inside edge; for a zipped opening leave it in one piece.

2   Inside back: pin to the side and top edges of the chair back. Make a dart around the thickness of the back if the corners are square, or pleat a rounded corner. Cut a rough curve at each bottom edge so that the muslin will fit around the back and along the line where the arm joins the back, avoiding the tuck-in allowance. Pin the muslin to the inside back of the chair around these curves and the bottom edge. Finish and clip the fabric. Pin the two back pieces together around the top and sides as for the bedroom chair.

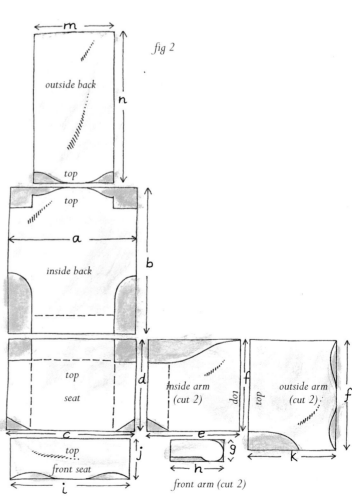

fig 2

3 Seat: fold over the tuck-in at the inside edge and sides temporarily, and pin the muslin to the four sides of the seat *(fig 3)*.

4 Inside arm: pin one inside arm piece to the right arm of the chair, so that the seam allowance on the top edge overlaps the widest point of the arm and the front arm. Pin and cut to match the curve on the lower inside back, then pin the tuck-in to the side of the seat tuck-in. Cut away a triangle at the front corner of the tuck-in *(fig 4)*.

5 Outside arm: pin the top edge to the top edge of the inside arm, keeping the lower edge parallel to the floor. Pin the back edge to the edge of the chair, and then to the lower edge of the outside back.

6 Seat: the shaping of the seat can now be completed. Pin the top edge to the lower edge of the back. Fold the corners inward, and pin the surplus fabric into two darts, forming an inverted box shape. Trim the seam allowance to ¾". This box should now tuck neatly down around the edges of the seat.

7 Front arm: pin to the front arm, keeping the grain straight, then pin to the inside and outside arms *(fig 5)*. Ease in any fullness; for a very curved arm you may need to make a few small darts in the main arm pieces.

8 Front seat: fold in half, then pin in place along the bottom edge of the seat and front arm, and the lower edge of the outside arm. Trim the hem around the cover so that it is level with the floor.

cutting out the main fabric

1 Trim seam allowance on toile back to ¾" and notch two or three sets of balance marks on each edge so the pieces will match up exactly. Unpin and press.

2 Plan the layout before you cut out the pieces. If you are using a patterned fabric, center any large motifs on the seat and back. A directional design should always be upright – this is why the arms are cut in two pieces – and must line up across the whole chair so that one side is a mirror image of the other.

3 Cut out the ten main pieces, using the muslin pattern, and transfer the notches. Also cut out eight 3" x 20" ties and a strip of fabric 6" x the length around the lower edge of the chair cover to face the scalloped edge. As a final check, pin each piece, right side up, to the chair, then pin the seams in the order in which they will be stitched. Adjust as necessary.

making the cover

Unpinning each piece as it is required, pin and sew the cover with right sides together, making a ¾" seam. Pipe the seams (see p.141) where indicated.

1 Sew darts on the top corners of the inside back, then sew the lower edges to the inside arms, double-stitching to reinforce the curves.

2 Sew a line of piping to the top of the outside arms, then stitch to the top of the inside arms, using a zipper foot. Cut away ¾" of piping cord from inside its casing at each end of the seam, so that the next seam will lie flat against it. Join

fig 3

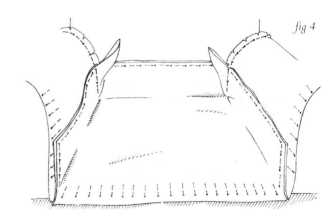

fig 4

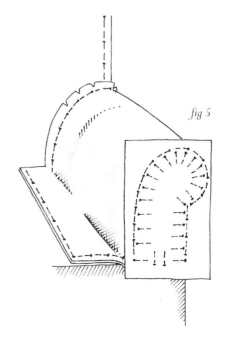

fig 5

the corners of the tuck-in on the seat, then sew the seat to the lower back and inside arms *(fig 6)*.

3 Pipe around the top and sides of the arm fronts, again removing the end of the cords, then sew in place. Pipe the top edge of the front seat and sew to the bottom edge of the seat and the sides of the outside arms.

4 Make a ⅜″ double hem on the inside edges of the two back pieces. Overlap and stitch the top 1¼″ together by hand and sew a line of piping across the top and down the sides. Pin and stitch to the front of the cover using a zipper foot. Turn right side out and press. Make the ties (see p.144) and sew on in pairs, one on each side of the back opening every 10″. If the chair has a plain back, leave three-quarters of one side seam unstitched and insert a zipper.

5 Zigzag the top edge of the facing and pin to the bottom edge of the cover with right sides together. Chalk a series of shallow scallops on the facing, reaching to within ⅜″ of the edge. Stitch along this line, and trim the surplus fabric, making a ⅜″ seam *(fig 7)*. Clip the curves, turn the facing to the wrong side, and press.

variations

If the seat projects in front of the arms, make allowance for this by extending the seat cover. A chair with a separate seat cushion will require a shallower tuck-in, and a fitted box cover for the cushion.

A sofa is, in effect, a very wide chair and a slipcover can therefore be made in a similar way. A separate skirt, which can have a plain or scalloped edge, can be cut in one or four pieces. The main cover will need to be cut to finish at the top of the chair legs and then a line of piping can be sewn around the lower edge before attaching the skirt *(fig 8)*.

fig 6

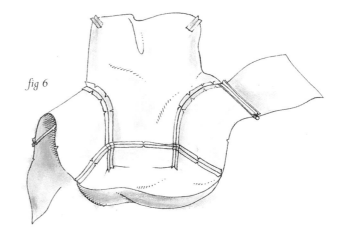

fig 7

fig 8

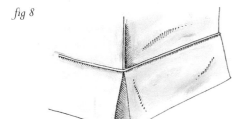

footstools

A matching footstool is a fanciful, although not necessarily essential, accessory for a covered chair. It is, however, a practical way to use up any leftover fabric. Here are two versions, one made from a simple rectangle, the other with an extravagantly gathered and ruched skirt.

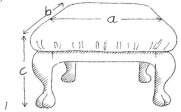

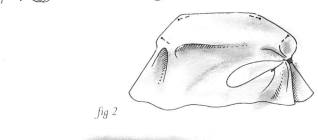

fig 1

slipcover with bows

materials

Main fabric, tailor's chalk, saucer, 48″ of 2″-wide ribbon (length 12″)

measuring & cutting out (fig 1)

Cut a rectangle, width = a + 2c, depth = b + 2c

Draw a curve at each corner, using the saucer as a guide, and cut to this line

making

1 Trim to neaten the outside edge, then turn up a ⅜″ hem all around. Center the cover over the stool and pin to the top at the corners. Make a pleat on each side of each corner so the fabric fits tightly over the padded top, and secure with a few stitches *(fig 2)*.

2 Cut the ribbon into four equal lengths and tie into bows. Trim each end into a swallow's tail. Sew one bow firmly to each corner.

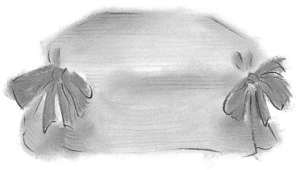

fig 2

ruched cover

materials

Main fabric, 2″-wide fringe (length = 3a + 3b), button thread

measuring & cutting out (fig 1)

Top: cut one, width = a, depth = b, + ⅝″ all around

Skirt: cut one, length = 3a + 3b, width = 2c, + ⅝″ all around

making

1 Join the two short ends of the skirt with right sides together and press the seam open. Make a ⅜″ double hem around the lower edge. Sew on the braid so the edge is level with the hem fold and ends join neatly. Make a zigzag gather (see p.142) ⅝″ from top of skirt and pull up thread to two-thirds of its length.

2 With right sides together, pin the ruffle to the top, distributing the gathers evenly (see p.142). Stitch down ⅝″ from the edge and clip into the seam allowance for a neat corner.

3 For a ruched look, make two pleats 2″ apart at each corner of the skirt, and catch together with a few invisible stitches *(fig 3)*. If the footstool has decorative feet, make the skirt short enough to show them.

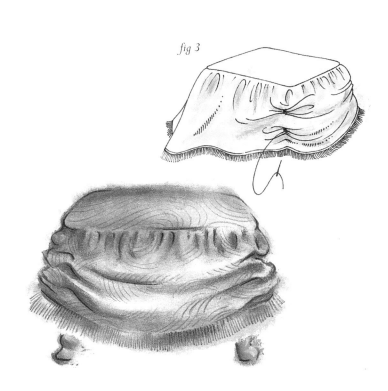

fig 3

bed dressings

Bed coverings are straightforward and relatively quick to make. Only the most basic sewing techniques — straight seams, hems, and gathers — are involved, although the scale is larger than you may be used to. A new quilt cover in a cotton print or a throw-over bedspread in heavier decorating fabric will instantly transform your bedroom, and a coordinating dust ruffle will complete the effect. See pages 155-60 for how to make pillowcases and pillow covers to match.

throws

Throws are very versatile – they can be made to any size, and in almost any fabric, from brocade to fake fur. Small rectangular throws may be draped over the back of a chair or sofa, while larger versions serve as picnic blankets or bedspreads. A reversible throw is put together using the bagging method described on p.143 and can be given a backing of quilted fabric for extra warmth. A single-sided version is made in the same way as the rectangular tablecloth on p.184. Fringe, braid, binding, or a narrow ruffle can be added to trim the edge.

tie-on quilt cover

The basic construction for this cover is the same as for the Decorative European Housewife pillowcase on p.155. Choose sheeting or extra-wide cotton to avoid any seams.

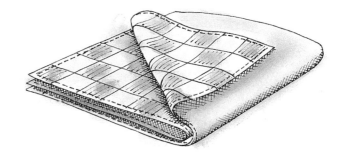

fig 1

materials

Main fabric, contrasting fabric for flap and ties

measuring & cutting out *(fig 1)*

Front: cut one, width = a + 1¼", length = b - 2"

Back: cut one, width = a, length = b, + ⅝" all around

Flap: cut one, width = a + 1¼", length = ¼b + 4"

Ties: cut six, width = 3", length = 21"

making

1 Sew a 1½" double hem along one long edge of the flap. With right sides together, pin the opposite edge to one short edge of the back, and stitch together along the seam allowance. Double hem one short edge of the front. Sew the other short edge to the unsewn end of the back, with right sides together.

2 Pin the front to the back along the sides, with the flap lying between them *(fig 2)*. Sew together, double stitching to reinforce the corners Trim the seam allowance to ⅜" and zigzag to finish. Turn right side out and press.

3 Measure the flap and divide into four. Place three pins along the hemmed long edge to mark the quarters. Make the ties as on p.144. Stitch three to these points along the hem line and three to the corresponding positions on the top *(fig 3)*.

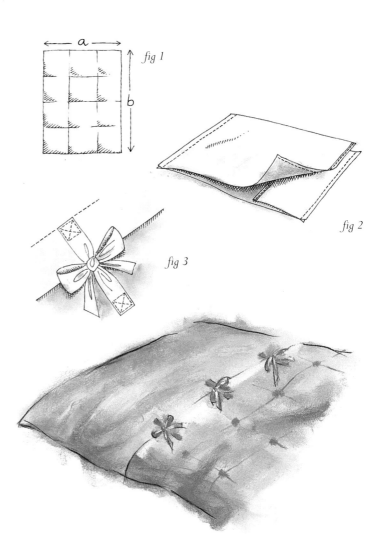

fig 2

fig 3

dust ruffles

A dust ruffle fits under the mattress to disguise the base of a bed. When working with expensive fabric it is more economic to cut the center of the panel from lining, and sew on a border of the main fabric. A line of piping can be added, between the ruffle and the panel, to either of the ruffles shown.

gathered dust ruffle

materials

Main fabric for ruffle (and panel border if required), lining fabric for panel

measuring & cutting out (fig 4)

Plain panel: cut one, width = a, length = b + ⅜", + ⅝" all around.

Curve the bottom corners to fit the shape of the bed if necessary

Bordered panel: from lining, cut panel center, width = a - 12",

length = b - 6"; from main fabric, cut one bottom strip,

width = 6", length = a - 12", and two side strips,

width = 6", length = b, + ⅝" all around each piece

Ruffle: cut one, width = 2c, length = 2a + 4b, plus ⅝" all around

making

1   To make a bordered panel, stitch the bottom strip to one short edge of the center panel with right sides together. Press the seam open. Sew the side strips to the long edges and press open. Curve the corners to fit the bed base if necessary. Make a ½" double hem (equal turns) along the top edge.

2   Fold the ruffle in half lengthwise and join the side seams. Clip the corners, turn right side out, and press. Attach to the three unhemmed edges, follow the method on p.142 *(fig 5)*.

box-pleated dust ruffle

materials

Main fabric for ruffle and panel, lining fabric for panel, contrasting fabric for inserts

measuring & cutting out

Panel: as for the Gathered Dust Ruffle

Side ruffles: cut two, width = c, length = 1⅓ x b, + ⅝" all around

Bottom ruffle: cut one, width = c, length = 1⅓ x a, + ⅝" all around

Corner inserts: cut two, width = 8", length = c, + ⅝" all around

making

1   Make the panel as for the Gathered Dust Ruffle. With right sides together, join one corner insert to each end of the bottom ruffle, then join the side ruffles to corner inserts. Make a ¼" double hem along lower edge and ends of ruffle.

2   Clip into the seam allowance at the center top edge of both corner inserts. Fold the sides of the ruffle pieces to the center to make box pleats and pin. With right sides together, pin the ruffle ends to the top corners of the panel and center pleats at the bottom corners. Pin down the rest of the ruffle in a series of 4" box pleats, 6" apart *(fig 6)*, then stitch in place ⅝" from the top edge.

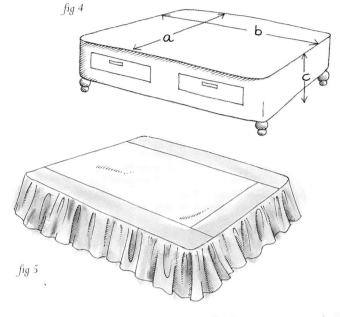

fig 4

fig 5

fig 6

table linen

A tablecloth, or even a set of coordinating table linen, is a simple project for a beginner, but one which has immediate visual impact. A contrasting square can be draped over a full-length round cloth in a bedroom, while a floral cover for a buffet table, with a plain rectangular cloth underneath, could be the focus of a celebration meal. See p.143 for how to join lengths of fabric to make a large cloth.

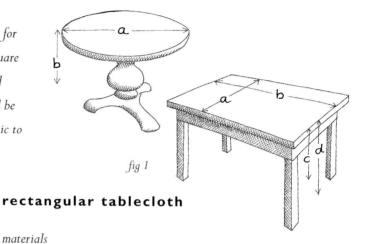

fig 1

tablecloths

Consider how the cloth will be used when deciding the length of the overhang. A decorative cover may skim the floor, but a kitchen tablecloth should not be longer than the seats of the surrounding chairs. Decorative fringing or binding can be added to the hem of a cloth of any shape.

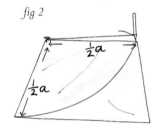

fig 2

round tablecloth

materials

Main fabric, paper, pencil, string, thumbtack

making the template (figs 1 & 2)

Cut a square of paper with sides equal to the radius of the cloth – ½(a+b) plus ⅝″. Tie one end of the string near the point of the pencil. Pin the other to a corner of the paper, so that the string is the same length as the side of the square. Keeping the string taut and the pencil upright, draw a quarter-circle curve. Cut out.

measuring & cutting out

Cut a square of fabric, with sides equal to a + 2b + 1¼″. Fold into quarters and pin the pattern through all four layers, matching the corner of the pattern to the folded corner of the fabric. Cut along the curve.

making

Sew a line of staystitch ⅝″ from the edge. Press the seam allowance to the wrong side, so that the stitching lies just inside the fold. Turn under and baste down half the remaining allowance. Hem by hand or machine.

rectangular tablecloth

materials

Main fabric

measuring & cutting out (fig 1)

Cut one rectangle, width = a + 2c or 2d, length = b + 2c or 2d, plus 2″ all around

making

Press under ¾″ along each side, then a further 1¼″. Unfold and miter the corners (see p.140). Baste and stitch the hem.

fitted buffet tablecloth

materials

Main fabric

measuring & cutting out (fig 1)

Top: width = a, length = b, + ⅝″ all around

Skirt: width = d + 2⅛″, length = 3a + 3b + 1¼″

Bow: (make four)

Main part: width = 10″, length = 14″

Center: width = 6″, length = 8″

Tails: width = 10″, length = c + ⅜″ all around

making

Join the two short edges of the skirt with right sides together and turn up a ¾″ double hem (equal turns) along the lower edge. Attach to the top following the method on p.142 to make sure the gathers are even. Make the bows as on p.144 and sew one firmly to each corner.

napkin

A simple square napkin is made from a 20″ or larger square of fabric. Finish the edges with a double ⅜″ hem, mitering the corners if preferred.

quilted table mat

Mats provide protection for a polished tabletop, as well as completing a table setting. They are a good way of using up any fabric left over from a tablecloth.

materials
Main fabric, batting, backing fabric, ruler, chalk pencil

measuring & cutting out
Front: cut one from main fabric, width = 16″, length = 12″
Back: cut one from backing fabric, as front
Batting: cut one, as front
Binding: cut a 2″ bias strip, 55″ long

making

1 Mark two lines on the right side of the front piece, from corner to corner, with a chalk pencil. Draw a series of lines, 2″ apart, which are parallel to these, so that the whole top is covered with a grid *(fig 3)*.

2 Sandwich the three pieces together, with the marked front and the back facing out and the batting in the middle. Baste from corner to corner, then around the outside edge, keeping the layers smooth. Work several more rows of basting parallel to the long sides, roughly 4″ apart.

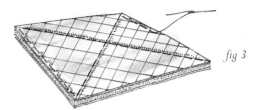

fig 3

3 Stitch over the marked lines, then remove the basting and round off the corners of the mat. Bind the edges as on p.140.

picnic roll

This rolled-up mat and flatware holder is ideal for a picnic.

materials
Main fabric, contrasting fabric, 2¾″-wide ribbon (length = 1yd)

measuring & cutting out
Outside: cut one from main fabric, width = 20″, length = 14″
Inside: cut one from contrasting fabric, as front
Pocket: cut one from main fabric, width = 12″, length = 8″

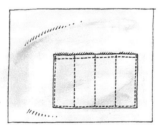

fig 4

making

1 With right sides together, pin the two main pieces together. Stitch, ⅜″ in from the edges, leaving a 4″ opening along one side. Turn right side out and close the opening with slip stitch. Press.

2 Turn under a ⅜″ double hem along the top of the pocket, and press under ⅜″ along the other three sides. Pin to the lower right-hand corner of the inside, 2″ in from the edges. Topstitch along the sides and bottom, ⅛″ from the folded edges. Divide the pocket into four equal sections with vertical lines of stitching *(fig 4)*. Always stitch in the same direction to keep fabric smooth.

3 Trim the ends of the ribbon on a slant and fold in half. Sew to the outside, two-thirds of the way down and 4″ in from the right-hand edge.

index

acknowledgments

I would like to thank everyone who has helped me to produce House Beautiful's Seasonal Guide to Decorating with Fabric - spiritually, mentally and physically!

Pippa Rimmer, Carl Braganza and Clara Thomas, my loyal, good-humored and ever-supportive assistants. Anna Lallerstedt, Valerie Howard, Elizabeth Brower, Kerry Woodbridge, Lauren Henry and Sue Rowlands, who were generous enough to let us disrupt their lives by allowing us to photograph their beautiful homes.

Fabric companies and crafts people, who have all contributed with their work: Melanie Williams, Lillimore Jacobson, Sue Ralston, Cover Up Designs and The Loose Cover Company. A very special thank you to all the fabric manufacturers for their generosity in supplying the fabric.

I greatly enjoyed being associated with such professionals as Jane O'Shea and Mary Evans at Quadrille, who made this book possible. Francoise Dietrich for her elegant and brilliant page design. Lucy Naylor for her much needed additional prose. Lucinda Ganderton for deciphering all the projects and writing the instructions, and the illustrator, Alison Barratt, for her exquisite artwork. Ellen Liberles for her painstaking work double-checking all how-to material. Alexa Stace, my editor, for staying calm over ever-changing pages. Francine Lawrence for believing in me and suggesting my name to the publishers. Last, but not least, my dear friend and photographer Pia Tryde, whose individual style and personality shine through every photograph. And, of course, a big hug for my lovely husband Pierre for putting up with me in moments of stress and always being at hand when needed - especially loading and unloading the car before and after photographic shoots.

photographic acknowledgments

The publisher thanks the following photographers and organizations for their permission to reproduce the photographs in this book.

2-3 William Shaw; 5 top center Simon McBride; 5 bottom Clay Perry; 6 Jan Baldwin; 8 top Jan Baldwin; 8 bottom Simon McBride; 19 top left William Shaw; 20 left Henry Bourne; 23 top center Jan Baldwin; 42 -43 Frank Herholdt; 43 top right Pia Tryde; 43 bottom center Pia Tryde; 44-45 Simon McBride; 44 left Elizabeth Zeschin; 48 bottom right (inset) David George; 49 top left (inset) Frank Herholdt; 49 top center (inset) Pia Tryde; 58 Jan Baldwin; 59 top Jan Baldwin; 59 bottom right Elizabeth Zeschin; 61 top left Jan Baldwin; 62-63 David George; 72 left Pia Tryde; 72-73 David George; 73 top right Andreas von Einsiedel; 73 bottom right David George; 74 top left Christopher Drake; 74 top right Jan Baldwin; 75 Jem Grischotti/The Sofa Workshop; 76 top left Tom Leighton; 76 top right Andreas von Einsiedel; 76 center left Frank Herholdt; 76 bottom left Frank Herholdt; 77 Frank Herholdt; 79 bottom center Charlie Colmer; 84 top right (inset) Jacqui Hurst; 85 bottom right (inset) Leonard Smith; 85 bottom left (inset) Jacqui Hurst; 101 top right Mike England; 101 bottom Thomas Dare 'Multi' collection, 341 Kings Road, London SW3 5ES Tel: 0171 351 7991; 108-109 Clay Perry; 114 top left Jan Baldwin; 114 bottom right Pia Tryde; 117 top left Pia Tryde; 117 bottom right David George; 118 David George; 119 top left David George; 119 bottom left and right Fran Brennan; 122-123 Pia Tryde; 123 bottom center Pia Tryde; 132 Christopher Drake; 133 top left Pia Tryde.

Special photography of all other images by Pia Tryde.